Delighted by Discipline

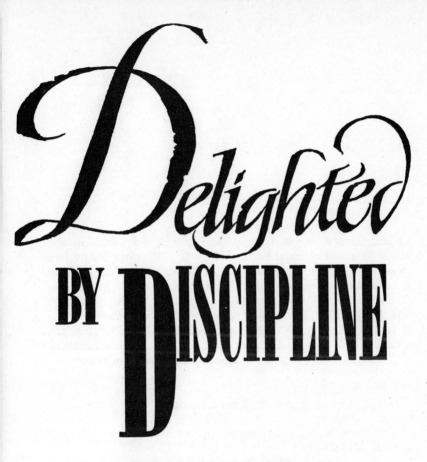

Delighted BY DISCIPLINE

MARK R. LITTLETON

While this book is designed for your personal reading pleasure and profit, it is also intended for group study. A Leader's Guide with Reproducible Response Sheets is available from your local bookstore or from the publisher.

VICTOR BOOKS®

A DIVISION OF SCRIPTURE PRESS PUBLICATIONS INC.
USA CANADA ENGLAND

Library of Congress Cataloging-in-Publication Data

Littleton, Mark R., 1950–
  Delighted by discipline / by Mark Littleton.
    p.   cm.
  Includes bibliographical references.
  ISBN 0-89693-792-5
  1. Bible—Study. 2. Bible—Devotional use 3. Bible—Memorizing.
I. Title.
BS600.2.L52   1990
220'.07–dc20
                                                          90-36998
                                                              CIP

1 2 3 4 5 6 7 8 9 10 Printing/Year 94 93 92 91 90

Dedication

TO
The Faculty of Dallas Theological Seminary
who first taught me
to apply the Scriptures to all of life.

Contents

Introduction

I have a tendency that troubles me. It's the tendency to forget what a joy Bible meditation, Bible study, and Bible teaching can be.

I say, "can be" because though it's not always a joy—sometimes it seems like a slog through ooze as thick as wet snow—I find that once I get into it, it frequently turns into something riveting and exciting, even thrilling. Insights and ideas flash onto the screen of my mind. Suddenly I see a connection of a verse to an event in my life ten years ago. Or there's that jolt of understanding in which I realize a principle applies to the very problem I'm facing now. Those little bolts of light and insight make it all worth it. I get to the point where I feel as though I have to grab someone and tell them, "Guess what I learned from the Lord today?!"

Most of the time I restrain myself, and that's probably wrong. Nonetheless, there's something down inside me that's bubbling up startling revelations of truths I never saw before, truths that relate to life's difficult problems, tense feelings, and broken emotions. When that happens, it's like a long ski down a beautiful mountain trail with the crisp wind biting your cheeks. As I carve flowing swathes in the snow, I look back to see where I've come from with a shout of jubilation in my heart.

Yet, it's not always that way. Sometimes I get so involved in something—writing a book, preparing a message, or working on a project—that I get caught up in the process and overlook the happiness there is in simply sitting at Jesus' feet.

Remember the story of Mary and Martha recorded in Luke 10:38-42. Martha was vexed and angry because she had to run about getting all the frills ready, while Mary sat at Jesus' feet listening to His teaching. While Martha was worried about whether the Lord's beefburger was medium rare, Mary was lapping up truth about the poor in spirit and those hungry for righteousness.

Still, I'll admit it, I tend to be a Martha. "Do something constructive," is my motto. Too often, just reading and imbibing Scripture doesn't seem "constructive." I want to accomplish something significant that lasts. Studying the Bible seems too much like a fruitless endeavor. The Scriptures don't even promise us a special reward for how much we read during our lifetimes. But there are plenty of promises about "good deeds."

Nonetheless, every now and then I go back and remember those first days of faith, when I became a Christian in August, 1972. I was twenty-one years old. Before my conversion I had been reading the Bible for some six months. It made no sense; nothing connected. I'd read ten verses, but the whole time my thoughts would drift. The words would sift through my sieve-like mind and when I was finished I'd feel relieved—"Well, at least I tried!"

Then I met Jesus. His light and life flooded my being. I felt as though some warm, glowing jewel had been placed deep down in my heart. From there it radiated warmth, communion, friendship, forgiveness, acceptance, and kind understanding out through my entire being. It was an excitement greater than anything I'd experienced and difficult to describe. At any moment I anticipated that Jesus might bolt down out of heaven in front of me and shout, "Come on, let's run a mile together and talk!" I envisioned Him there with me everywhere I went.

I remember picking up my Bible during that time and simply reading. I was astonished. For the first time I understood what it said. I knew that the One who had given us those words was with me, inside of me, around me. Every particle of His creation was shot through with kindly wisdom, profound insight, and gentle understanding. It was as though I saw Him in everything, especially His Word. When I read the Bible something deep down inside told me that God Himself was speaking to me. It was the truth I had been seeking for years; it was the answer.

I read hungrily, eagerly, desperate to devour every delicacy that seemed to emanate from the pages of the Word. Every new truth was a firecracker discovery. Every promise seemed to explode in my mind, saying, "This is yours. It's from Jesus to you. Believe it. Let it color your outlook. Let it change your life." I gripped those words, took them with me when I worked putting in fences, walked down the sidewalk, and browsed through the Sears racks. Everywhere I went His truth seemed to speak quietly and softly in my mind, assuring and encouraging me.

The Right Words at the Right Time

I remember a significant incident that happened in those early days. My grandfather had suffered a stroke, and my grandmother was understandably distraught. Everything was going wrong for her. Though she had been a devout believer all her life, she felt betrayed, confused, and hopeless.

My mother asked me to stay at Grandma's house for awhile to try to comfort her. One night, in the early morning hours I awakened, suddenly aware of her quiet weeping and sobbing in the next room. I didn't know what to do. But I had been memorizing Scripture, reading the Word, struggling to understand and apply everything to life around me. I thought the Lord might be able to help even if I couldn't.

But what would I say to her? I didn't know.

Still, something had to be done. I got up, walked to her bedroom, and knocked. She invited me to come in. I asked her what was wrong, and she poured out her feelings. "It's the end, honey. It's really the end. Nothing will go right from now on. I wish it would just be over. I wish the Lord would take us all home."

She looked at me through sad, blurry eyes, and I felt like crying myself. What could I say? Grandpop had been felled by a stroke. He was paralyzed. We were putting him into a nursing home. Some were even talking about selling the house they'd lived in for over fifty years. It did look like the end.

But I silently prayed and asked the Lord to give me the words. Moments later, Proverbs 3:5-6 was in my mind. I had memorized it only days before. "Trust in the LORD with all your heart and lean not on your own understanding; in all your ways acknowledge Him, and He will make your paths straight." I quietly quoted the verse, then explained, as best I could, what it meant and how it could apply in her situation.

Gradually, her crying ceased. She looked at me surprised, still sniffling, then said, "Where did you learn to preach like that?"

I didn't know. I wasn't a preacher. I had been a Christian for less than a year.

We talked for nearly an hour. She kept saying how she'd

never heard the Bible explained like that. Finally, she thought she could sleep.

The next day on our rounds we visited a friend. She said to her, "You should hear that grandson of mine preach. Last night he explained a piece of Scripture better than I ever heard in church. It was so simple. He's really something."

As I felt a lump of gratitude grip my throat, I quietly thanked the Lord. His Word did have power.

Traveling with the Word

Another time, I was traveling home at Christmas break from seminary in Dallas, Texas. It was my turn to drive, from 1:00 to 6:00 A.M. There were five of us in a big Pontiac Bonneville. I wondered how I could keep from falling asleep. Everyone else was snoring.

I tried singing quietly, listening to the radio, and going over class notes in my mind. Then I hit on the idea of meditating on a passage of Scripture. Since it was Christmas, I chose Luke 2:1-7, describing Jesus' birth in Bethlehem. I wasn't sure how to start, so I simply began trying to put myself into the passage, striving to imagine what must have gone on. It started out with the decree of Caesar Augustus.

My mind began firing questions at the passage. Why did Luke start with that? What was so important about the decree? Why did Caesar even issue a decree?

My thoughts roved among various possibilities. Suddenly it occurred to me that the Scriptures foretold that Jesus had to be born in Bethlehem. Joseph and Mary were from Nazareth. God had to get them to Bethlehem. How?

I was astonished. He chose Caesar to issue a decree about a census! But it made sense. If God is sovereign, if everything spoken of in the Word connects and reveals truths about Him, then this was one more piece in the puzzle. The Lord Almighty motivated Joseph to travel to Bethlehem by starting with Caesar Himself.

"But why?" I wondered.

Again, I discovered answers. What if this was God's way of saying He had charge over everything? Moreover, what if this was His way of assuring us that even the decrees of kings and potentates can be used in His plan? What if, above all, this was God's way of stripping big men down to size? That is, Caesar made thousands of decrees in his life. But only one was important—the one that touched on the life of Jesus Christ! And Caesar probably signed fifty bills that day, with this one at the bottom of the pile!

I don't know if my judgments are true, but believe me, it was 3:00 A.M. and I was as wide awake as I can get. I plunged along through the passage, pulling out insight after insight. In the end I found myself singing, "O Little Town of Bethlehem," to four sleepy seminarians wondering what on earth had happened to their driver.

In the preceding years there have been many experiences like the two above—memorable, rejuvenating, uplifting, challenging little stops in the race of life when I've had a chance to sit down at Jesus' feet and listen.

In the process, I've discovered that Scripture contains vistas and continents of wisdom so vast we can never fully tap its lode. The treasure is like a pile of jewels a hundred miles wide and high. And each jewel, once you've held it and owned it, bursts with new beauty and radiance as time goes on.

It's the claiming of those jewels that this book is about. I don't pretend to know everything about Bible study and meditation. But I do know some things that I have found useful, even thrilling. I hope that as you continue, you will enter into those realities and begin mining treasure that only emperors can dream about.

One

SOLVING
YOUR
PROBLEMS
SUCCESSFULLY

A peasant woman lived with her husband and two children in a very small hut in Russia. It was already crowded, but then her husband's parents lost their home and came to live with them. Conditions were unbearable.

She had heard of the village's wise man, how he had always solved the worst of problems. She went to him and asked, "What shall I do?"

"Do you have a cow?" he asked.

"Yes."

"Bring him into the hut, then see me in about a week."

A week later, she returned. "It's more unbearable than ever."

"Do you have chickens?" the wise man asked.

She did.

"Then bring them into the hut and see me in a week."

The woman couldn't believe this was the wisest man in the village, but she obeyed. In a week she was back. "It's an impossible mess. Cow dung all over the place. Chicken feathers flying. And people, people, people."

"Fine," said the wise man. "Now take out the chickens."

She did and reported the next week that things were much better.

"Now," said the wise man, "take out the cow. That will certainly settle your problem."

She did. And everyone lived happily ever after.

I don't know that you'd consider that a matchless piece of wisdom for overcrowded living conditions, but it was a remarkable way of attacking the problem.

In a similar way, Christians at the end of the twentieth century struggle with problems that defy the wisest of minds. Even as I write I'm aware of a number of problems people of faith are facing. Cancer. Divorce. Children into drugs. Raging in-law disagreements. Pregnancy out of wedlock. Guilt over having an abortion. Desertion of a family.

Where is there hope and help? Some would answer, "The Bible" or "Jesus." But that can be like saying the answer to longevity is eating garlic and onions. The Bible is a big book. You can get lost in it very easily. Jesus is in some ways a mysterious person. The very fact that He claims to be in charge over all things can be the very thing that drives many from Him. "You mean He allowed this?"

Wisdom, Insight, And Understanding

It's in this context that I often remember a series of verses in Psalm 119. "Oh, how I love Your law! I meditate on it all day long. Your commands make me wiser than my enemies, for they are ever with me. I have more insight than all my teachers, for I meditate on Your statutes. I have more understanding than the elders, for I obey Your precepts" (vv. 97-100).

These verses speak of some of the riches that spring from God's Word. As you read them, you can see several interesting developments in that series. For one, there's the movement from wisdom to insight to understanding.

What are these realities? What can they do for our lives?

Next, you notice four different types of subject matter: law, commandments, testimonies, precepts. Again, what are these and how are they different? What difference will they make for our lives?

In addition, you see the shift from enemies to teachers to "the aged." Three different groups and types of people. What is their significance?

Finally, you see four different actions. He meditates on the law all the day (v. 97). God's commandments are "ever mine," and for that reason he has greater wisdom than his enemies (v. 98). Again, God's testimonies are "my meditation." That's what gives him insight beyond his teachers (v. 99). And then there's the "understanding" element he's gained through "observing" God's precepts (v. 100).

Are these all different ways of saying the same thing? Or are they powerful realities, each of which can transform, enhance, and enrich our lives?

I believe the latter is the answer and that through gaining an understanding of these truths we will grasp something of the treasures Scripture has to offer. In this chapter, we'll look at these commandments that make him "wiser" than his enemies.

Overcoming Wisdom

The "commandments" that made the Psalmist wiser were God's injunctions, laws, and truths that tell us how to conduct ourselves. They refer in particular to the "you shalls" and "you shall nots."

That's simple enough. But what kind of wisdom do these commandments give? Perhaps we can come at it by asking what wisdom is not. First, wisdom in Scripture is not necessarily common sense. However, common sense is often built on wisdom, so the two can't always be separated.

Moreover, biblical wisdom is not that shrewdness that knows how to get its way in a selfish world. We might call that cunning or "worldly-mindedness" or even pragmatism, but it's not necessarily wisdom.

Nor is wisdom simply the gleanings of experience, as one worldly wise man put it when he was asked how he got so wise: "I've got good judgment. Good judgment comes from experience. And experience—well, that comes from having bad judgment."

Finally, biblical wisdom is not merely knowledge—collecting, separating, and analyzing the facts. One can have knowledge without wisdom, though he cannot have wisdom without knowledge.

What Is Wisdom?

What then is biblical wisdom? For one thing, it's endowed by the Spirit of God. "For this reason, ever since I heard about your faith in the Lord Jesus and your love for all the saints, I have not stopped giving thanks for you, remembering you in my prayers. I keep asking that the God of our Lord Jesus Christ, the glorious Father, may give you the Spirit of wisdom and revelation, so that you may know Him better" (Eph. 1:15-17).

Second, it gives us the ability to walk in a manner that pleases the Lord. "For this reason, since the day we heard about you, we have not stopped praying for you and asking God to fill you with the knowledge of His will through all spiritual wisdom and understanding. And we pray this in order that you may live a life worthy of the Lord and may please Him in every way: bearing fruit in every good work, growing in the knowledge of God" (Col. 1:9-10).

Third, it enables us to choose the excellent way, not what is good or better, but what is best. "And this is my prayer: that your love may abound more and more in knowledge and depth of insight, so that you may be able to discern what is best" (Phil. 1:9-10).

Ultimately, wisdom means knowing God and His ways and being able to apply His truth to the problems and situations of life. In other words, it's a skill in applying God's truth to life. It's goal is pleasing God above all, not itself or others. The wise man approaches life from the standpoint of, "What would God have me do in this situation?" And if he's not sure precisely what God would say, then he asks, "On the basis of what I know about God and His ways, and considering that His Spirit dwells within me, what do I believe He would have me do in this circumstance?"

True wisdom, then, is from God, for God, and through God. It's not generated from humanity. That's why common sense—which must naturally come from a depraved, renegade spirit—can never approach true scriptural wisdom.

That's not to say, however, that common sense is useless or foolish. In many matters, especially in the area of inventiveness, practicality, and the solving of mechanical or scientific problems, common sense is very useful. Thomas Edison applied common sense to daily problems and came up with life-improving inventions like the phonograph and light bulb. Amazed at his so-called "inspirations," someone asked him the source of his imaginative creations. He said it was "99 percent perspiration" and only "1 percent inspiration."

When he fought for weeks, going sleepless for days at a time, to find a filament that wouldn't burn up in the vacuum tube he was using to create the light bulb, he was asked if he'd found a way. He replied that they knew "one thousand ways *not* to do it." Common sense is often the simple process of discovering what works after many trials and errors.

But biblical wisdom is concerned with moral and spiritual matters, not practical invention. It doesn't work on the basis of trial and error, but on the basis of revelation. God tells us the best way at the outset. We don't have to fail to get it right.

That's one reason that while our world has advanced in giant steps technologically, we remain in a moral malaise. We have abundant common sense for solving mechanical, electrical, and biological problems. It's the personal ones that get us. And they're what wisdom is all about.

The World And Wisdom

James contrasted the worldly way with godly wisdom. He said that the kind of worldly wisdom that produces selfish ambition and jealousy is "earthly, natural, demonic" (James 3:15, NASB). What are those things?

Earthly means "earthbound," concerned only with this world and getting along in it. It's ultimately self-centered. It leaves out God who created us and this world.

Natural could also be "sensual." The idea is that it seeks only to satisfy the sensual longings. Again, it is selfish and unconcerned about others or God.

Finally, it's demonic—straight out of the pit and Satanic world that presently fights against God with lies.

But what is true wisdom? James put it this way. "For where you have envy and selfish ambition, there you find disorder and every evil practice. But the wisdom that comes from heaven is first of all pure; then peace-loving, considerate, submissive, full of mercy and good fruit, impartial and sincere" (3:16-17).

Look at those qualities:

- ■ Pure—free from selfish, sensual inclinations; objective and honest.
- ■ Peace-loving—promoting healthy relationships.

- Considerate—not pushy, willing to wait; recognizing that others may not agree immediately.
- Submissive—flexible; not stubborn, willing to listen and be open.
- Full of mercy and good fruit—caring about the needs of others, especially those who suffer.
- Impartial—unwilling to compromise the truth no matter what; not to be bribed, or agree for unjust reasons.
- Sincere—without hypocrisy; it never says one thing and does another.

What is most astonishing here is that Christians—all of them—have access to and can possess this wisdom, simply by asking for it. "If any of you lacks wisdom, he should ask God, who gives generously to all without finding fault, and it will be given to him" (James 1:5).

Solving Problems

Wisdom then, is the mental, emotional, and spiritual ability to solve problems successfully. Those problems fall into two areas: personal problems, and the problems of others. Let's look at them a little closer.

Wisdom is above all the ability to solve *your* problems. Have you ever heard of a marriage counselor who's been divorced? Or an investment counselor who's flat broke? If they couldn't solve their own problems, why should we think they can solve ours?

In a way, it's not such a dilemma. People can be objective and helpful in viewing others' situations, but they can be desperately foolish about their own.

Personal problems are the hardest to solve. Even Paul said, "For what I do is not the good I want to do; no, the evil I do not want to do—this I keep on doing" (Rom. 7:19). He recognized that while he knew what was right, getting it right in his own life was supremely difficult.

But true wisdom can and does solve personal problems. When I first became a Christian, I engaged in a desperate struggle with swearing. Though I whipped the problem verbally, my mind remained embedded in the "curse-response." I heard the words in my head, even if I didn't say them with my tongue. It was unnerving, exasperating, and guilt-inducing.

Then I heard a preacher speak on how memorizing the Word of God and meditating on it could drive out evil thoughts. He described a woman who tried to grow grass in the desert. She failed repeatedly, except in one spot — the little area under her kitchen window where she threw out the dishwater. That daily douse in dishwater made grass grow. Similarly, that preacher said, your mind will produce healthy, godly thoughts as you douse it daily in Scripture.

I applied this principle, and it began to work. Today, my mind rarely echoes those ugly thoughts that once were an aggravating conditioned response.

Others' Problems

Wisdom also helps you solve others' problems. Remember the two prostitutes who were brought to Solomon in a dispute over the death of one of their children? (1 Kings 3:16-28) One night, one of the mothers switched kids. No one could solve the problem of who was telling the truth. But Solomon did by suggesting that they cut the living child in half and give half to each mother. The real mother was then revealed by her unwillingness to kill the child.

Solomon could solve others' problems. In fact, the whole Book of Proverbs is his sourcebook of wisdom for how to live life. How many people have kept from evil ways and foolish decisions through reading his words?

The crazy thing is that while Solomon provided us with

some of the best wisdom in heaven and earth for solving problems, he couldn't solve his own. He ended up a wretched idolater and lost the kingdom for his sons.

A Little Deeper

The wisdom we're talking about here goes deeper. It confounds ones enemies. "Your commands make me wiser than my enemies" (Ps. 119:98). Why does the psalmist put it that way? Why didn't he say, "Your commandments make me wiser than the great sages"? Or, "Your commandments make me wiser than my Dad ever was"?

Wisdom is moral skill for dealing with problems successfully. While a teacher or a pastor might pose some rather sticky problems, it's your enemies who will give you the worst time of all. While Parliament gave Winston Churchill some dandy difficulties during World War II, it was Adolph Hitler who gave him the worst clouts of all. While President Carter struggled with some awful internal messes during his presidency, everyone will agree that the Ayatollah Khomeini still managed to throw the worst wrenches into his work.

Your enemies will always pose the worst problems for you, because their goal is to knock you down and out. If they don't get you the first time, they'll come back for a tenth and twentieth. To have wisdom greater than your enemies is a compelling comfort.

But more than that, the Psalmist's comparison here is of the wise man using God's wisdom against his enemy using worldly wisdom. That is why the commandments make him wiser—because he has truth and God Himself on his side.

Jesus Blew Them Away

Jesus' enemies continually tried to trap Him into saying or doing something that would compromise His commitment to God and the truth. Thus, they fired some of their best (and worst) shots at Him in debate.

One of the worst situations is found in John 8:1-11. In that story, the Pharisees hurled a woman caught in the act of adultery at Jesus' feet. Then they said, "In the Law Moses commanded us to stone such women. Now what do You say?" They wanted to see if Jesus would contradict Moses' Law and thus discredit Himself in the eyes of the people.

But there was a second problem here. If Jesus did tell them to stone her according to Moses' Law, He would also get into trouble with the Roman authorities, for no one could administer capital punishment but them.

It was a shrewd dilemma and the Pharisees knew it. If Jesus said, "Yes, stone her," He'd be approving Moses' Law, but the Romans would take Him away. If He said, "No, forgive her," then He would be going against Moses' Law and thus lose His integrity. Jesus was not only impaled on the horns of this dilemma, He appeared about to be gored to death by an angry crowd. There was no escape.

What did Jesus do? He said, "If any one of you is without sin, let him be the first to throw a stone at her."

Whoa! What a shot! It was a left hook, and the challengers were left reeling. He had upheld both Moses' teaching and His own with one deft whack of logic and truth. God's commandments had made Him wiser than His enemies.

A Jab To The Ribs

Another instance of Jesus' wisdom came from a challenge, this time by both the Pharisees and the Herodians. It's found in Mark 12:13-17. Here, the supporters of Herod—the political wags of the Romans, and the defenders of the Law, the Pharisees (who, by the way, were archenemies with the Herodians up until this point), approached Jesus about a ticklish problem of their day: taxes. They gave Him some fine words about how He was partial to no one and always taught God's truth, then they put out their net: "Teacher, we know You are a man of integrity. You aren't swayed by men, because You pay no attention to who they are; but You teach the way of God in accordance with the truth. Is it right to pay taxes to Caesar or not?"

This was a hotly argued issue every day in the market place. The Jews believed God had given them the land of Israel. Therefore, to pay a tax to Caesar was recognizing that Caesar was the king. It was, in their minds, a form of blasphemy to God. Moreover, Caesar was worshiped by the Romans as a god, and paying tribute to him in this way was regarded as a kind of recognition of his sovereignty over them. This turned taxpaying into idolatry.

But the problem for Jesus was worse. If He said, "No, don't pay," then the Herodians could trounce Him as a rebel and traitor. But if He said, "Yes, pay," then He could be in violation of one of the Ten Commandments that said, "You shall have no other gods before Me" (Ex. 20:3). What could Jesus do? It was a cunning trap and it appeared that He was done for.

But no, again knowing the wisdom that comes from God's commandments proved its superiority over Jesus' enemies. He asked for a coin and held it up, then said, "Whose portrait is this? And whose inscription?"

"Caesar's," they replied and probably had an inclination to spit the word in contempt. Then He said, "Give to Caesar what is Caesar's and to God what is God's."

Where was this Man from? How could He escape so easily, and with such sense? Easy, He had the wisdom which comes from meditating on God's Word. Once more, that wisdom enabled Him to jab the Pharisees in the ribs and knock them flat.

A Whole Flurry Of Punches

But the best example of all was the temptation scene in the wilderness with Satan (Luke 4:1-12). Here, Jesus faced the most formidable, cunning, and intelligent enemy in history. How would He fare?

Each time Satan tempted Him, Jesus replied with a commandment of God, "It is written." There was no argument, no assembling of briefs, no back and forth. One word from God, and the trickery was tripped headlong off a cliff.

Three times Satan tried to trap Him. Three times Jesus answered from the Word. Three times Satan was riddled with the bullet holes of heaven.

It was knowledge of, meditation on, and the ability to apply God's commandments that gave Jesus the victory over Satan. Had He tried to argue on human terms, or even begun to reason along with Satan, He might soon have found Himself in agreement. But God's commandments locked the brakes. There was no other way. Jesus had God's wisdom on the problem of food when you're hungry, how to win fame and honor, and whom to worship. God's commandments made Him wiser than His enemy.

What's The Point?

God's wisdom, gained from meditating on His commandments and His Word, gives us skill for solving even the most difficult problems of life. Be it divorce, communication in marriage, raising children, healing relationships, overcoming bad habits—God's Word has answers for those who will meditate on it.

Where then does wisdom come from? Again, Scripture has the answer: through a healthy fear of God. "The fear of the Lord is the beginning of wisdom, and the knowledge of the Holy One is understanding" (Prov. 9:10). The fear of the Lord involves reverence for His authority, respect for His person, obedience to His commandments, a hatred for all sin and evil, and a holy awe in His presence. There is nothing in nature akin to it. It is man in relation to Creator. It is how we stand before Him. That fear grows as we grow.

One of C. S. Lewis' Narnia stories speaks of how Lucy, one of the children in the tales, comes upon Aslan, the lion who represents Christ. She hasn't seen him for a long time. But the moment she happens upon him, she's stunned and says, "You're bigger."

Aslan replies, "That is because you're older, little one."

She says, "Not because you are?"

He answers again, "I am not. But every year you grow, you will find me bigger."[1]

So it is with fear of God. As we grow, we find Him bigger. And bigger. And greater. And more magnificent than ever. With Him comes that perfect wisdom showing us the way to solve our problems.

Getting The Fear That Leads To Wisdom

How do we gain this fear of God that leads to such wisdom? Solomon provides a statement in Proverbs 2:1-5 (NASB):

■ "My son, if you will receive my sayings . . . "
The first thing is to receive God's Word. "Faith comes from hearing," Paul said (Rom. 10:17). Accept it. Believe it. Receive it.

■ ". . . and treasure my commandments within you . . . "
Treasure them. That's a sure word. Hide them in a place where they'll be safe, untarnished, and available on need. You gain this fear through treasuring God's Word as your highest possession.

---

[1]C.S. Lewis, *Prince Caspian* (New York: Collier Books, 1951), 136.

■ " . . . make your ear attentive to wisdom, incline your heart to understanding . . . "

Again, you make your ear attentive—your mind alert and receptive—by concentration, openness, willingness to spend the time. You incline your heart by stopping all other activity and giving it your complete attention.

■ " . . . for if you cry for discernment, lift your voice for understanding . . . "

Cry out for it. Pray for it. Ask God to help you see it. This is a determined, "nothing-will-stop-me-in-this" kind of crying. It's an absolute commitment.

■ " . . . if you seek her as silver, and search for her as for hidden treasures . . . "

Again, seeking, searching, going to the ends of the earth if necessary to get this thing you desire.

■ " . . . then you will discern the fear of the Lord, and discover the knowledge of God."

How do you get the fear of God that leads to wisdom? Follow the pattern from Proverbs 2:

1. Receive His commandments.
2. Treasure it within you.
3. Listen to Him.
4. Cry out for it.
5. Seek it.

Do these with all your heart, soul, mind, and might. This fear of God will cause you to meditate on and love His Word beyond all other principles, truths, books, or sayings of this world. When you do that, you shall be on the road to possessing God's wisdom—forever and always.

There's treasure to be had. The first kind is wisdom—the ability to solve your problems successfully. You gain it only by going after it with all you have. But it's not all there is, more treasure lies ahead. Keep seeking and you will learn to be *delighted by discipline*.

Two

GETTING
BENEATH
THE
SURFACE

I was recently reading William Manchester's fine book about Winston Churchill, *The Last Lion: Alone, 1932– 1940*. Manchester details Churchill's life in those perilous days before World War II when he stood virtually alone in forecasting what Hitler was about to do.

What fascinated me was the fact that Churchill repeatedly warned everyone — in newspaper columns, in Parliament, in other writings — that Hitler was not a man of peace. But Churchill went unheard, and even scoffed at and hated.

But what is even more fascinating is the reader looking back at what now appears to be obvious and inevitable. How was it that Churchill could see ahead so well, while others, in even higher positions and possessing perhaps greater intelligence, failed?

Manchester brings much of the answer out in his history. Churchill spent his entire morning, every day, reading all the major newspapers in London. He scrutinized the editorials and searched out every fact, studying it to see what was behind it. After that came the stack of mail, sent in from every quarter — from an admirer in Greece to the

Prime Minister himself. He pored over it all, grasping at some hint of significant truth in various places.

Each afternoon and evening he entertained guests, many of them nobility, many world travelers, who informed him in the process of conversation about events the world over.

But he paid special attention to the news, dispatches, speeches, and letters from Germany. He watched what was going on in that country with a keen, steady eye.

In the evening his research assistants poured into his office and he began to compose the various pieces of writing he was working on—from the speeches he'd make in Parliament to a short comment for the New York Times. He labored over the words, rewriting them constantly till the phrase turned. Sometimes he wept, sometimes he laughed over his own verbiage. From his office flowed a steady stream of important, memorable statements to the world he sought to influence.

Churchill, as one of the world's greatest political statesmen, possessed a quality few leaders ever gain: insight. He was able to see the meaning and significance of things, from a dropped word in a conversation, to a tone pattern in a speech, to what a country or nation was feeling. As early as 1924 he wrote that the German nation was looking for an opportunity to avenge itself after the indignity of Versailles and the results of World War I.

Another Brand

Churchill, though, did not have spiritual insight, but political insight. His expertise lay in the area of "seeing inside" in a political and earthly sense.

There's another kind of insight, similar to this, that Scripture speaks of. It's used in Psalm 119:99: "I have more insight than all my teachers, for Thy testimonies are my meditation" (KJV). The word used here for insight refers to depth of knowledge, an ability to see within and behind the scenes. Understanding the meaning and significance of something gives us the picture.

For instance, Nehemiah 8:8 indicates the teachers of Israel taught the people from God's Word, "They read from the Book of the Law of God, making it clear and giving the meaning so that the people could understand what was being read."

"Making it clear" there is the same word for insight. In other words, the teachers paraphrased the Scriptures and translated them from the Hebrew into the Aramaic of the day. They spelled out, illustrated, and illuminated their meaning. The people understood what the words really meant and thus could use them in their lives.

Another helpful passage is Psalm 32:8, "I will instruct you and teach you in the way which you should go." David meant that he'd give highly specific directions. He'd have "his eye" upon his students. That is, he'd give them the instruction, then watch to see if they truly understood by their actions.

Daniel sought insight from God in understanding some of the visions he'd received. Daniel 1:17 (NASB) says that God gave the four youths—Shadrach, Meshach, Abednego, and Daniel—"intelligence" or insight in "every branch of literature and wisdom." That was in-depth knowledge. It wasn't superficial at all. They saw things through to the heart.

In Daniel 9:22, the prophet speaks of how Gabriel the messenger angel gave him instruction, saying, "Daniel, I have now come to give you insight and understanding." Gabriel would reveal to him the whole plan of future history. Daniel would see as no man had seen. He was given revelatory "insight."

Thus, insight is the ability to learn a subject:

■ in-depth

■ with a constant eye to its significance and meaning
■ so that you understand it in truth (in reality).

There's no superficiality here, no pretense or bombast.
You see the truth. You know it's the truth. And you trust it
to guide you in your conduct and thinking forever after.

How is insight different from wisdom? Wisdom has a
"problem" orientation. That is, it concerns itself with solving problems.

Insight, on the other hand, has a "purpose" or meaning
orientation. It understands what motivates people, what
lurks in their hearts, what lies beneath the surface. It sees
the meaning and significance behind events. It can "read
between the lines," and like the proverbial watchmaker, it
understands what makes things, people and nations tick.
Insight gives one the ability to look into the eyes of the
person and see what goes on inside. It is essential to anyone who seeks to understand God, His people, and any
other subject under the heavens.

Insight Into What?

A person may gain insight normally in three areas. The first
is self. You gain insight into your own being, personality,
motivation, and thought processes.

For instance, there was a man whose son had a demon.
Jesus' disciples tried to cast it out, but they couldn't. Then
Jesus arrived on the scene and the man implored Him.
Jesus said to him, "Everything is possible for him who
believes." Immediately, the boy's father exclaimed, "I do
believe; help me overcome my unbelief!" (Mark 9:23-24)

That's a potent little piece of insight. The man looked
within himself and saw his problem with faith, that it was a
mixture of hope, belief, unbelief, doubt, and despair. He
was desperate, but he was also honest.

Paul was another man of insight. His exposition of the

struggle of good and evil within a man in Romans 7 is not only revelatory, but insightful. He recognized that while he knew the truth, he didn't always do it. What was the solution to this dilemma? Jesus. His insight led him to greater faith and dependence on the Lord.

An interesting contrast was Peter's lack of insight into himself. When Jesus told him in Luke 22:31-34 that he would deny Him three times before the cock crowed, Peter became proud and insistent that he could never do such a thing. But he had little insight into his own motives and problems with cowardice. He failed to listen to one who was giving him insight into himself.

Insight Into Other People

Secondly, we can gain insight into others. We see beneath the surface of looks, expressions, and statements to what they're really thinking and doing. When Peter exposed Ananias and Sapphira in Acts 5, he was led through the power of his Spirit-led insight. He saw the truth of their motives and their deception.

We find another example in Jesus' encounter with the rich young ruler (Mark 10:17-22). He wanted to know how he could inherit eternal life. Jesus ultimately replied with stern insight. He saw that the young man had a problem with covetousness and love of money. He provided a solution, but the man wouldn't listen and went away unsaved.

Insight Into God

The third area of insight concerns Jesus and God. We can gain insight into the Lord's mind through His Word. How many times have you read some passage in the Bible and come away struck with some new truth about God? That's insight. The Spirit, at that moment, is opening your mind to new truth—new to you, but perhaps old to others.

I have always enjoyed reading in the book of Job. I have wondered for years why God never told Job the immediate reason for his suffering, which was Satan's attack. On the contrary, God even took responsibility for the whole thing, asking Job if he had the wisdom to tell God how to run His creation. Why did God handle it like this?

It's an insight that I gained, I believe, through reading: God wants us to trust Him, not fear Satan! He desires that we understand all things are in His hands, even Satan, and all events are ordered by Him, even if He is never the cause of evil. Thus, God's purpose was to lead Job back to complete trust and confidence in Him. He didn't bring Satan into it, because that would cloud the issue.

It made me realize again that God desires that we fear no one but Him in this world and that we trust no one in a final sense, but Him. I admit, that's probably not a world-shattering insight, but it strikes fire with me. Such thoughts can come, though, every time we read the Bible. God is eager to give us insight and wisdom, far more eager than we may be to receive it.

More Insight Than My Teachers

But there's something more here. In Psalm 119:99, the psalmist says that he has more insight than all his teachers. Was this man boasting, claiming to be a genius, or giving us a way to trounce those professorial types who inhabit our lives?

The reason he has this insight is because "Thy testimonies are my meditation." It's not that he has greater insight necessarily than godly teachers, though that's possible, but that he has more insight than worldly teachers who neglect the Word of God. He has greater depth in spiritual and moral matters than any of them.

Three Examples

There are three potent examples of this kind of insight in Scripture. The first is Joseph. He was cast into prison supposedly for molesting his master's wife (which was false). There, his insights were so keen that he soon ran the whole prison. On one occasion, he interpreted two dreams that Pharaoh's cook and cupbearer had. The dreams came true, but the cupbearer failed to report it to Pharaoh.

Later, Pharaoh had his own dream in which God told him about the events of the next fourteen years. All the wise men of Egypt tried and failed to interpret the dream. It was then that Joseph was brought in and successfully interpreted it under God's guidance. Joseph concluded with the words, "And now let Pharaoh look for a man discerning and wise, and set him over the land of Egypt" (Gen. 41:33).

Though the Hebrew words used here are different from the one used in Psalm 119:99 for "insight," the idea is the same. Joseph advocated putting a man of insight over the land, to guide and direct affairs so that the famine did not destroy the people. Clearly, Joseph, because of his commitment to the Lord, possessed greater insight than all his teachers.

The second example is Daniel. In Daniel 2 a similar situation to that of Joseph existed. The king had a dream and all his ministers tried to find out what it was. But the king wouldn't reveal the dream, for it was a test. Anyone could make an interpretation, but the one who could reveal the dream would be special. Daniel was brought in and confounded everyone by revealing the dream and its interpretation.

The third example is Jesus Himself. In Mark 12, He is approached repeatedly by the teachers and leaders of Israel who seek to trap Him, or at least find Him in error on some point. After a number of deft rebuttals, a scribe asks Him which is the foremost commandment (vv. 28-34). Jesus replies with a quote from Deuteronomy 6:5, the Shema of Israel, which commands us to love God with all our heart, soul, mind, and might. He adds another command from Leviticus 19:18, which tells us to love our neighbor as ourselves. The scribe answers that Jesus is correct, and adds that following those two commands is greater than all burnt offerings and sacrifices. Jesus then replies, "You are not far from the kingdom of God" (v. 34).

It's at this point that all questions cease. No one could trap, undermine, disprove, or disqualify Jesus' insight. He had more insight than all His teachers.

The Source of Power

Psalm 119:99 (KJV) concludes, "Thy testimonies are my meditation." The Ten Commandments were often called the "testimony." They were God's solemn charges to His people, His commands, and laws of life. Throughout history, by meditating on God's Word, people have gained insight into all matters under heaven.

Some years ago, I counseled with a married couple. The wife had had an affair and I was trying to help them work through it to find real forgiveness and future fidelity. The husband had gotten to the point where he had wanted to march into "the other man's" office with a gun and shoot him. "He took something from me!" he cried.

I was struck by his words, and, at that time, as an unmarried person, by what effect infidelity has on a relationship.

But he went on, "I just can't shake this anger, this jealousy. I don't know what to do. My wife has changed, and she won't do it again. But there's so much anger."

Instantly, my mind reached back to a passage in Proverbs. I opened my Bible and found it. I said, "You know, your feelings are exactly what the Bible says you'd feel. Let me read." I then read Proverbs 6:32-35: "But a man who commits adultery lacks judgment; whoever does so destroys himself. Blows and disgrace are his lot, and his shame will never be wiped away; for jealousy arouses a husband's fury, and he will show no mercy when he takes revenge. He will not accept any compensation; he will refuse the bribe, however great it is."

I came back to those words, "jealousy arouses a husband's fury." My friend stared at me, astonished, "That's exactly what I feel. Nothing she or that man could do to try to make it go away will help. You mean that's in the Bible?"

I nodded and told him that faith in Jesus and forgiveness were their only source of hope. Unfortunately, he was not, at that time, ready for it. But I came away again astounded at how the Scriptures give insight into the character of human life.

Insightful Power

It's the Word of God that gives this insight. Through meditating on and understanding it we reap tremendous dividends including the ability to give help to people in need. Now when people raise a problem, I find myself turning to the Scriptures immediately. "The Bible says something ✶ about that," has become my byline. For it's the Word of God that offers us grist for the mental mill. It's the Word that throws light on the reality around us. Without it, we're traveling through darkness with no light in sight.

In William Shirer's book, *The Nightmare Years*, he (like the earlier book on Churchill) offers an eyewitness history to the events that led to World War II. Shirer was a reporter in Europe who covered many of the situations in Germany during the rise of Adolph Hitler. Since I have read littleabout World War II, I was astonished how often Shirer demonstrated that Hitler's tactics were built on bluff, deceit, and bullying. I couldn't help making mental comparisons of Hitler to the personality of Satan as revealed in Scripture. Over and over, I found exact parallels to Hitler's behavior.

For instance, there was the passage in 1 Peter 5:8 (NASB) where it is said that Satan "prowls about like a roaring lion, seeking someone to devour." The reason a lion roars is to scare his prey into submission, for the lion knows he's not as fast as the prey. In fact, lions prey mostly on the sick and dying, not the living.

Hitler, like that lion had a far bigger roar than a rear guard. Shirer points out that he would have lost many times in his early confrontations with the British and French if they had not backed down so easily. In fact, the first year of World War II on the Western Front saw little action. Hitler was busy in the east trouncing Poland, Denmark, and the Scandinavian countries. His west flank was open and vulnerable, but neither Britain nor France took the opportunity. They seemed fixed in a holding pattern. Hitler's roar had frozen them with fear and virtual volitional paralysis.

Still, this insight convicted me personally in other realms. I began to see how I myself would try to bluff people into submission by making a loud roar! I saw it in business relationships, and even in my own home. It was startling (and convicting).

Insight Into A Personal Problem

In another context, I noticed that when I disagreed with someone—especially family members—mild words quickly escalated into angry ones and we'd soon be embroiled in a real verbal brawl. It seemed like it couldn't be stopped.

I prayed for insight. The Spirit led me to a verse in Proverbs, "A gentle answer turns away wrath, but a harsh word stirs up anger" (15:1). It became a source of transforming insight. Conflict escalates into argument because people begin slinging hot words at one another. Soon they're at virtual fisticuffs.

But I began applying the Proverbs passage. When an angry employee marched into my office with some verbal garbage, I simply listened and tried to give a gentle answer. When he continued his furious way, I still supplied the gentle answers. And then what? Lo and behold, he looked at me and said, "How come you're not mad at me?"

In the family, I tried the same thing. Suddenly, my child didn't seem to get so upset—and I didn't have to raise my voice. And my wife and I actually had a disagreement without a single angry stomp off into the sunset.

These kinds of insight can multiply with every verse of Scripture that the Christian memorizes and applies. They become like the round stones David used to slay Goliath. With them we slay the falsehoods and untruths that inhabit our world.

The Price Of Insight

How do you get such insight? Again, this book is about the whole process. But you have to go back to Psalm 119:97: "Oh, how I love Your law! I meditate on it all day long." Notice those words, "all day long." That means exactly what it says. Remarkable! Yet it doesn't seem possible. How can you meditate on the Bible all day long?

I have found that it is possible in this sense: the preoccupation of your mind becomes the Word of God—if you work at it and apply the principles Scripture sets forth.

I frequently think of one of the things Dr. Howard Hendricks told us in seminary one day. He spoke of how Dr. Donald Barnhouse was on a plane reading his Bible. A theology student sat nearby, reading *Time* magazine. But he recognized the great Bible teacher and finally sidled over for an exchange of words. He asked Dr. Barnhouse, "What can I do to become as great a communicator of the Bible as you are?"

Dr. Barnhouse took a searing look at the *Time* in the student's hand, and said, "Son, as long as you're reading *Time* magazine, you'll know more about it than this book!"

Insight comes at a price. But it's one that one can pay easily—just by opening the Book and reading on.

Three

PUTTING
IT
ALL
TOGETHER

Many years ago Dr. Chaim Weizmann and Professor Albert Einstein shared a Zionist mission together on a ship bound for America. Upon arrival in New York, the reporters asked Dr. Weizmann how he and Einstein spent their time. "Throughout the voyage," Dr. Weizmann answered, "the learned professor kept on talking to me about his theory of relativity."

"And what is your opinion about it?"

"It seems to me," Dr. Weizmann replied, "that Professor Einstein understands it very well."

The ability to understand, to comprehend something complex (or even simple) often eludes us. Of course, in the area of the Theory of Relativity few of us would fail to smile at Dr. Weizmann's reply. Yet, how often in human relations have we cried out for that measure of insight and understanding that would make everything clear? If we only knew more of the facts, we could solve anything. But so often a few of those facts are missing, and our understanding is hampered.

The psalmist says "I have more understanding than the

elders, for I obey Your precepts" (Ps. 119:100). This kind of understanding about life, God, the world, and self is critical to one's success in dealing with the problems of life effectively. But what is understanding?

The Nature of the Beast

Wisdom involves the ability to solve problems in a skillful and practical manner. Insight gets beneath the surface, sees the meaning behind things. It grasps motives, desires, needs. It reads between the lines. But understanding reaches another, perhaps higher level altogether.

There are a number of Hebrew and Greek words that we translate into the English word "understanding." From them, though, we can distinguish four elements of this important concept.

Everyday Comprehension

The first is comprehension, the ability to understand the meaning of a statement or action. Frequently I'll use a word and my five-year-old daughter will say—a week later—"What does such and such mean?" I can't even remember the context, but she insists I said it. So I come up with a definition. Occasionally, she'll ask something more difficult though, like, "Why is water wet?" "Why do we use towels?" "How come Mr. Smith has such a big belly?" And, "Why are babies little?" (My wife just had our second child.)

Answers to these questions in some respects require comprehension of her meaning. What's she really asking? Understanding involves more than the words themselves, but what the real meaning is behind the words. In some ways, this crosses over into "insight," as there is a mixture of meanings here. But in this area understanding is crucial.

A person of understanding sees beyond the superficial definitions to the meaning behind them.

For instance, I recall a time when my daughter had been crying a lot, bursting into tears about the slightest irritations. One morning I noticed my wife and I had been paying a lot of attention to our little baby. That same morning Nicole ran downstairs crying. I asked her what was wrong. She said something in the bathroom scared her. I asked her what. She was obviously groping for something. Finally, she said, "I turned around and the towel scared me."

The towel? I didn't know they were that malignant! But then I looked behind the words. She needed some reassurance. Her real fear was that we didn't care anymore about her. She thought the baby had supplanted her in our hearts. I gave her a long hug and some gentle words. In a few minutes, her tears were forgotten and she was playing and humming to herself, happy and relaxed.

Nehemiah spoke of such understanding in Nehemiah 8:13 when the people gathered around to "give attention" to the Law: "On the second day of the month, the heads of all the families, along with the priests and the Levites, gathered around Ezra the scribe to give attention to the words of the Law." They sought to understand.

When Philip approached the Ethiopian eunuch in Acts 8:30, he said, "Do you understand what you are reading?" It was not only the actual definitions of the words that were necessary, but the intent behind them. He needed to comprehend with his mind and his heart.

Identification

A second aspect of understanding involves identification and empathy. You can see what another person is thinking and feeling. Because of your understanding you know how to handle a situation.

For instance, Proverbs 20:5 says, "The purposes of a man's heart are deep waters, but a man of understanding draws them out." In this case the man of understanding recognizes that someone has some thoughts or ideas that he's keeping far beneath the surface. It may be that he doesn't want anyone to know. Or perhaps he's afraid to tell for fear that others will reject or denigrate the idea. But a person who possesses true understanding knows the feeling and is able to draw the thoughts out of him, both by making him feel comfortable and accepted, and also by asking the right questions.

I remember visiting a professor for a personal conference when I was in seminary. I had an idea about a book, and I wasn't sure whether it was viable, nor was I convinced he wouldn't laugh at it. But I made an appointment with the idea of getting to know him better. I thought that if things felt right I'd tell him about it. But if not, we could talk about other things.

The conversation went well. We discussed school, my grades, how I was growing, what I was learning. Then he jarred me when he said, "But this isn't what you really want to talk about."

He waited for my reply, and I wasn't sure what to do. But the way he sat there so open and willing to listen, I finally laid it all on the table. He was instantly pleased. But then his real understanding came out. He helped me shape my thoughts and focus them so that my vague plan became blackboard-clear through our discussion.

The next day in class he referred to our conference without mentioning my name or idea. But he commented, "He shared with me an excellent idea. We put it under the microscope and got it in focus. I hope he follows through. Now my only concern is to keep him away from other Christians who will tell him his idea won't work and make him give up."

He was a man of understanding. He helped me draw out the deep water in my own soul.

There's another aspect of this, though, and it's that element of understanding which convinces others you really know what's going on inside of them. Keith Miller writes in his book, *The Becomers*, of how Paul Rees told him about a priest who ministered in a leper colony on a Pacific island. He couldn't get anywhere in telling them about Jesus. But then one day he discovered he had leprosy. Word filtered through the community. The next morning, his chapel was filled and many converted to faith in Christ. The lepers now knew he understood what they faced and how they hurt. They could identify with him. Now they could listen to his Gospel message.[1]

The Ability To Distinguish

A third element of this spiritual ability is the power to distinguish or discern among several possibilities and to choose the best and right course of action. In 1 Kings 4:29 we are told that God gave Solomon a spirit of "understanding." The word used there involves a root which means to "separate" or "distinguish." King Solomon had to make numerous decisions every day choosing between the ideas of his various counselors. How was he to discern which advice was the best and which option to take? His internal spirit of understanding offered him that power.

King Solomon's discernment of the two prostitutes fighting over the baby in 1 Kings 3 was also an indication of his understanding. He was able to distinguish among the many elements of what was happening and come to a fair and right conclusion.

This is also an indication that wisdom, insight, and

---

[1]Keith Miller, *The Becomers* (Waco, Texas: Word, Inc. 1973), 52.

understanding all go together. Like the three lenses of a microscope, they're all essential in the decision-making and problem-solving process.

The Gigantic Puzzle

However, I'm convinced that there's a fourth element of understanding that might even stand alone as the greatest capacity of all. What is it? I'd call it the ability to "put it all together." To make an invention work with unity, harmony, beauty, and simplicity all at once. To see beyond the individual trees to the whole forest. To get above the details of God's work in history and see the whole plan.

We see this reflected, for instance, in 1 Chronicles 28:9: "And you, my son Solomon, acknowledge the God of your father, and serve Him with wholehearted devotion and with a willing mind, for the Lord searches every heart and understands every motive behind the thoughts. If you seek Him, He will be found by you; but if you forsake Him, He will reject you forever." Here, God "understands" every intent of man's thought. He's able to put it all together into a unified whole and see where it has been, where it is, and where it's going.

Another example is Jeremiah 51:15: "He made the earth by His power; He founded the world by His wisdom and stretched out the heavens by His understanding." God stretched out the heavens on the basis of His understanding. Why did He make it the way He did? How is it that it all holds together, stars don't collide, and things remain in place while traveling all together at enormous speeds? Why doesn't the sun burn us up? Why don't we run the risk of spinning out of orbit? One reason: God's understanding. He was able to put it all together perfectly.

Proverbs 20:24 offers another side of this truth: "A man's steps are directed by the Lord. How then can anyone understand his own way?" Every step a man takes in his life is already ordained by God. God planned it ahead of time, marked out its limits, and orchestrated its movement. He's behind it all. If we could enter the mind of God and grasp His thinking on our lives we could then understand why everything has happened the way it has.

Unfortunately, such understanding is reserved, in some respects, for God alone. But on the other hand, the Christian, through the guidance of Scripture and the Spirit, can look back in hindsight on the events of life and put them together in a comprehensive whole that makes sense.

There have been life-shattering events in my life that have changed the whole direction of things. Over five years ago I went through a difficult church situation that led to my resignation. Not wanting to jump back into a ministry, I joined a secular business. At the time of the change, I was shattered, convinced God had allowed a terrible mistake. But looking back, I see how well it all fits. Through getting into a secular job, I have learned much about working with people, sharing my faith, and what the average business-person faces every day. But in addition, I had the opportunity to learn how to use computers and a word processor. Developing these skills sparked my writing ministry and led to my first four books.

That change of five years ago launched me rather than leveled me. Today, I'm still not sure about returning to a pastoral ministry. But I am sure that God "causes all things to work together for good," as Romans 8:28 (NASB) says.

This kind of understanding keeps Christians from becoming bitter and resentful over the events God has brought into our lives. All things are part of a beautiful tapestry, though we may not see the pattern at the time of the weaving, we can still look back and marvel at God's handiwork. How many times I've met people who are bitter and broken over the circumstances of their lives! Yet, if they sought true spiritual understanding, they'd be able to see God and perhaps His plan behind it all.

Understanding About What?

I see several things we are to "put together" in this respect. One is the overall plan of God for history. How many scholars have struggled to understand the unfolding of history? Aristotle, Thomas Aquinas, Arnold Toynbee, Eastern mystics, the Greeks—all these men and movements have burned to see the whys behind the whats. The Greeks came up with a cyclical view that history repeats itself in great circles every few thousand years. Others have called for a more linear progress, with everything supposedly getting "better and better." There's the theory of evolution, which posits other ideas about history. Then there's the communist system of history which works toward the classless society. The great names in the history of ideas—Hegel, Nietzsche, Marx, Freud, Jung—all have tried to explain why things happen the way they do.

But God has revealed the truth in one book—the Bible. The person of true understanding studies the Bible so that she may comprehend God's plan for Planet Earth. It's through that process that she comes to terms with the theological realities of Creation, Fall, and Redemption. Through the Bible we gain an understanding of why the Cross and Christ stand at the center of redemptive as well as world history. The Bible allows us to put it all together to see the big picture. It also allows us to see how our own era fits into history's timeline.

Thus, the person of understanding knows that human history had a starting point. She knows where it's going and why. She sees where her generation fits in. And she looks forward to the grand conclusion and the starting over.

Personal Plan

A second truth is a person's ability to grasp something of the meaning and plan of his own life. He not only sees God's grand plan, but he sees how he individually fits into it. He can set the reality of his own conversion, gifts, and purpose into context. He can gain a personal sense of significance through that understanding.

As I grow as a Christian I become more excited about the life God has given me. Though most of it has not progressed or developed according to my hopes and expectations, what has happened has been nothing less than a marvel. I have been through some periods of terrific personal pain. I have struggled through problems that defied every grain of wisdom I brought to them. I have at times despaired of ever accomplishing anything. Yet, I find myself ignited with a deep sense of adventure nearly every day. "What will the Lord bring into my life today?" has become my morning headline. At the end, I can nearly always reflect on something new learned, something transforming that happened, or something never before anticipated that draws me on to the next day. There's never any boredom in the kingdom of God.

Small Details

A third element of true understanding is the ability to put together a small detail of life and see the whole picture. At times, a problem crashes into my life that seems utterly inexplicable. I can't understand what is happening, much less why. But true understanding gives us the ability to gather the necessary facts, and like pieces of a puzzle, put them together so that we can see the best solution.

My job is the management of my business' customer service department. Recently, a follow-up problem that involved keeping track of over 100 parts orders befuddled me. I tried numerous ways of solving it, but each solution failed and the problem continued. It all involved consulting too many lists and files to keep a handle on things. I prayed about it and kept asking the Lord for insight.

Then one day I was looking at our magnetic "in and out" board that indicated where each employee was on any given day. The movable magnetic dots and squares made it easy to map out one's own itinerary as well as track someone else's.

Instantly, I saw the whole scope of the situation with tracking orders. I went to my desk, devised a tracking system, and it's now in place and working well. On one board I can keep in touch with over 100 orders, sources, and vendors that repeatedly stymied me before.

It's this ability to see the larger picture that a person of understanding possesses. You can apply it to other contexts, but you can see it's a critical concept. Without it, we have no sense of history, God, life, or self. It's what makes us fully human.

Wisdom Of Years

But a special element of understanding is referred to in Psalm 119:100 (NASB), the fact that the psalmist had greater understanding "than the aged." Why did he say it this way?

Because it's the aged person, the one who has "seen it all" who is best able to grasp the big picture. He's the one who understands the feelings of the young lad on his first date with a lovely girl. He's the one who can marshal more experience, wisdom, and insight for the solution of a problem. She's the one who through years of study, meditation, and reflection can dig more deeply into a truth than others.

This psalmist—even though young—has greater understanding than the older person. Why? Because "I obey Your precepts." Notice that it's the "obeying" of precepts—the rigorous application and determined use of them in the problems of life—that has given him this understanding.

Hebrews 5:13-14 recalls a similar thought. "Anyone who lives on milk, being still an infant, is not acquainted with the teaching about righteousness. But solid food is for the mature, who by constant use have trained themselves to distinguish good from evil." It's because of "constant use" that one has the ability to "distinguish good from evil."

How many times have you struggled to decide whether a certain course of conduct was right or not? To marry or not to marry? To embark on a career, or go into the ministry? To watch R-rated movies, or not? To go to dances, or play games, or drink alcohol—you name it—Christians have struggled with those realities.

Furthermore, there are the more exasperating decisions that seem to involve scriptural principles on opposing sides. For instance, I know what the Scriptures say about disciplining my child. One verse tells me to use the rod or I'll lose her. Another one says to bring her up in the "discipline and instruction" of the Lord. Still others tell me to be a servant, to be gentle, not to make her angry, to be consistent, and to be forgiving. How do you put all these ideas together? Where's the balance? Through understanding you can gain it by separating the elements, and seeing which exhortation applies to each situation.

On another front, how do you reconcile a passage which tells us to be a servant to others and at the same time keep from being a doormat and an abused person?

Or, how can you honor your parents, and at the same time love your spouse as Christ loved the church, when your parents and spouse may be in a severe personal conflict?

Or, how do you find the happy medium between sharing your faith with someone who rejects it, and just being a friend and loving them? How often do you speak of spiritual things? Where do you draw the line between personally offending them, and offending them because of the truth of the Gospel?

All these questions are answered by gaining biblical understanding and applying it to the circumstances. When you apply the truths in life you discover whether they accomplish their mission, or whether they falter and fail.

How Do You Get It?

You get this kind of understanding by "observing God's precepts" and applying His truth to the problems of life. Again, that's the whole purpose of this book—to help you learn to use the Scriptures in all of life and gain that wisdom, insight, and understanding that enables us all not only to survive, but to succeed in a spiritual way.

Perhaps Proverbs 9:10 says it best: "The fear of the LORD is the beginning of wisdom, and knowledge of the Holy One is understanding." The way to get understanding is ultimately the same: you start with the fear and knowledge of God. Once you have that firmly fixed in your heart, everything else begins to fit into the slots. You will soon learn the delights of discipline.

Four

IS BIBLE MEMORIZATION JUST FOR KIDS?

She was pretty. Tall. Brown hair. Pert. A certain coyness. Sophomore in high school. Maybe she had a slight crush. Her name was . . . . Well, actually I forget. It was a long time ago.

I had come out to her house with a girl I was dating. We planned to go horseback riding. But before we went out to ride, she sauntered up to me with a secretive look on her face. She said, "Would you check me out on my Bible memory work?"

I had worked on memorizing Scripture for several years, but I'd never had anyone "check me out." She explained, "It's a program we have at church. BMA. 'Bible Memory Association.' We memorize passages of Scripture. We have these little books. I have to give my verses this Sunday. I need someone to make sure I'm word perfect. Would you?"

I agreed. She recited her verses. She was, indeed, word perfect. I was impressed.

"You do this all the time?"

"Except the summer."

"You memorize these verses and recite them? What do you get for it?"

"Oh, there're all kinds of awards and stuff. It's just a program in church. I've made a lot of friends through it. Actually, I like it. It trains my mind."

"Trains your mind?"

"I don't know. Strengthens it. I've been a better student since I started doing this. It's helped me learn to be disciplined—mentally, I mean."

I was intrigued. It astonished me that a pretty high school sophomore would spend the time. But then, she had made plenty of friends.

I've known for years that the starting place to gain the wisdom, insight, and understanding we've been talking about is memorization of Scripture. But that brings up a question: Why memorize? When I met that teenager in the BMA so many years ago, I had to ask myself, Why did I memorize Scripture? Why was I so committed to it? What drove me so hard?

I remember when I first began memorizing Scripture. I became a Christian in the summer of 1972, after my graduation from college. The next year I decided not to blitz the business world with my presence, so I became a ski bum at Stratton Mountain in Stratton, Vermont. I was a short-order chef at breakfast, lunch, and dinner, and a maniacal skier the rest of the time. I loved it.

One day I received some information from a Christian campus organization. They enclosed a brochure with a listing of all their tools and books used in discipleship and witnessing. I decided to purchase a few. I combed through the list and noticed items that sounded perfect. Then I discovered a nondescript offering in the back: a "Bible Memory Pack." The blurb explained the secret and necessity of Bible memorization. So I added it to my already lengthy list of purchases. I sent off the list and a check.

Three weeks later I received several books, over a hundred tracts, and my Bible Memory Pack. I tore open the tracts and got ready for the slopes. I put the books on my shelf. But I gave the Bible Memory Pack a glance, then tucked it into my dresser drawer. "No need for this at the moment," I thought. I headed off for some ski wizardry.

I gave out my tracts to people I went up the lifts with. I was happy, whistling. But that evening, something was wrong. My mind seemed to whiz off to the sinful unknown. Lustful thoughts, swearing, and all sorts of evil ideas pummeled my brain until I had a roaring headache. I couldn't understand it. In the five months or so that I'd been a Christian, I had cleaned plenty of garbage out of my life. But now it seemed it was all sprouting up again in a virtual deluge.

The next day I felt more depressed. I was walking in my room, praying, when suddenly I said, "What on earth is wrong, Lord? My brainwaves have gone berserk."

It was then a thought resounded clearly in my head. "Remember that Bible Memory Pack you threw in the back of your drawer? Maybe you'd better get working on it."

I swallowed and nodded. I hadn't thought about it for two days. I rushed to my dresser, pulled out the pack, and read through the instructions. In an hour I was working on my first verse. That verse took me a week of determined repetition before it was firmly stitched into my mind. But I was on my way. That pack, and, later, other devices were to become a focal point of my spiritual life.

Words To Remember

I offer these two examples at the start of this chapter because I know how difficult it is to motivate people to memorize Scripture. Churches feature programs, pastors exhort, and disciplers encourage, but little memory work gets done. Our lives in the 1990s have become so helter-skelter that we feel frazzled and dazed, seemingly unable to concentrate on anything deeper than a situation comedy.

I once exhorted my congregation, "If you memorize two verses a week for a year, you'll have over a hundred verses memorized. If you do that for ten years, you'll sock away over a thousand. Now how many of you have been Christians for ten years and know by heart over a thousand verses?"

There were no hands raised.

"A thousand verses!" one man said to me. "I'm lucky to remember John 3:16." He tried to recite it and didn't even get that one right.

"Two verses a week," another lady said. "I've got the wash, a Sunday School class, a house to clean, and you want to pile it on some more? Forget it."

One man confessed to me, "My mind couldn't retain it, Mark. I'm just not that smart."

Some people have told me they'd have to have a photographic memory to be able to do such a thing. People haul out every excuse in the book. Yet, memorization of Scripture is one of the most critical elements of spiritual living.

The Shema of Israel, from Deuteronomy 6, was the first Scriptural passage a Jew memorized. He repeated it every time he came into his house, into the temple, and into worship. In it God said, "And these words, which I am commanding you today, shall be on your heart; and you shall teach them diligently to your sons, and shall talk of them when you sit in your house and when you walk by the way, and when you lie down and when you rise up" (Deut. 6:6-7, NASB). God's words were to lodge securely in the heart, never to be excised. A father who placed them on his heart would so overflow with their truth and goodness that he'd be teaching his sons everywhere he went. That was the idea. But few Christians do it.

Again, God spoke to Joshua and warned him, "This book of the law shall not depart from your mouth, but you shall meditate on it day and night, so that you may be careful to do according to all that is written in it; for then you will make your way prosperous, and then you will have success" (Josh. 1:8, NASB).

Notice what God commanded. The "book of the law" — that is, the books of Moses, the first five books of the Bible — "shall not depart from your mouth." The word "depart" means making a conscious effort to rid yourself of it — to let it slip away, to walk away from it and not turn back. It would be like taking the Bible and throwing it away, then walking in the opposite direction to get as far away from it as possible. Another idea would be refusing to speak of it or mention it. Have you ever met someone who has suffered a broken relationship and will not even refer to the other person again? That's the idea. You choose not to recognize it or refer to it. It's a conscious departure and break.

No, Joshua was not to let it depart. Rather, he was to meditate on it day and night. "Meditate" means to muse, to mull over, to think about it with the mind, to examine it. God's Word was to be a continual and present reality, so much so that it occupied his very thoughts.

Ask yourself, "How much do I think about God's Word and truth during the day?" Joshua was commanded to think about it constantly. There are numerous other verses in Scripture that speak of the need to know God's Word by heart. But maybe you find yourself offering excuses:

- I don't have time.
- My mind isn't good at memorizing things.
- I used to do it and it didn't work well.
- I've put in my time; I don't feel I need to anymore.
- I already know plenty of verses.

■ It's too hard.
■ I serve the Lord in other ways.
■ Who wants to carry around a little pack of cards?
■ I always forget to do it.

Ultimately, you have to be motivated by the Spirit and by your own fervent desire to please the Lord. One thing is sure. You can't do it for the wrong reasons, or ultimately you'll give up.

The Wrong Reasons

What are the wrong reasons? Let me offer you several.

1. *Because the group does it and demands it.* One man I know confessed to his businessman's group, "I was just memorizing new verses because I knew I'd have to recite one each Friday. I finally just stopped. I felt that was legalism."

He was right. If his only reason was to impress a group of men in his Friday Bible study, he was memorizing for all the wrong reasons. It couldn't last.

2. *Because you'll get an award.* Awards for children in Pioneer Clubs and Awana groups are strong motivators. But sooner or later you have to move beyond "lollipop motivation." Whether the lollipop is a little patch or a trip to Paris really doesn't matter. It's not the kind of motivation God desires.

3. *Because someone else did it whom you respect.* Maybe you want to be like someone who knows a horde of Scriptures. Fine, but you'd better find stronger reasons or you'll give up when that person ceases to be an important example for your life.

4. *Because the pastor said to do it.* The pastor may have said such a thing, but why did he say it? What truth was it based on? You have to get beyond the pastor and back to God's truth, or it won't last.

5. *It's sort of a family thing.* Traditions, family or otherwise, are great. But again, you have to get past them to the foundational reasons, the reasons for certain behavior as found in God's truth.

6. *Because I think it will make me more spiritual.* Indeed it will help you grow spiritually. But simply memorizing Scripture isn't what makes a person spiritual or mature. It's the application of Scripture to life that matters.

7. *Because I want to win arguments.* Strangely enough, some people memorize Scripture so that they can whip others in theological or evangelistic arguments. It's certainly wise to know what you believe and why, but becoming a "walking Bible concordance" is not the purpose of Scripture memorization.

The Right Reason

Why memorize Scripture? I can think of no better reason than God commands us to do it. And since we want to please Him we obey. It's as simple as that.

God commands it. Numerous verses throughout the Bible command us to store up His Word in our hearts. Joshua 1:8, Deuteronomy 6:5-8, Psalm 119:11, and Colossians 3:16-17 are a start. But the whole Bible is a treatise on the need to know God, His Word, and to obey.

Therefore, we'll do it. Obedience. Personally, I used to rebel at the idea of obeying simply because God says so. I used to think there were all sorts of better reasons to obey—out of love for the Lord or a desire to please Him. But when you get down to the pay dirt real obedience involves all those things. Moreover, when you gain the mentality of obeying because God says so, you rid yourself of much of the hemming and hawing that goes with so much Christian behavior. If we have to stop and think why God commands what He does every time we face one of

those laws, we become perfect targets for Satan's rational-
izations. The moment we depart from God's Word
(remember His words in Joshua 1:8?), we're open to a
direct assault from Satan.

God longs for obedience from His people more than
anything else. For through obedience, everything else—the
fruit of the Spirit, evangelism, spiritual life, freedom, victory—becomes possible. Obedience is the keynote, the key
chord to the music of heaven. It's the first step to any
other spiritual accomplishment.

By this I don't mean a blind sense of duty, doing things
out of fear of punishment. Rather, what must occur in the
heart of a believer is a transformation from obeying out of
fear of the consequences to obeying because He is good,
wise, and loving.

Anne Sullivan, in seeking to train the blind and deaf
child, Helen Keller, came upon this notion early in their
relationship. She wrote, "I saw clearly that it was useless
to try to teach her language or anything else until she
learned to obey me. I have thought about it a great deal,
and the more I think, the more certain I am that obedience
is the gateway through which knowledge, yes, and love,
too, enter the mind of a child"[1]

There's an old story about a discouraged minister's
dream in which he had the job of striking a piece of granite
with a pickax. He swung the ax for hours, but never
achieved so much as a dent. Finally, he gave up. The moment he stopped, a man stood by him and asked, "Weren't
you given this task? Then why are you stopping?"

The minister replied, "My work is in vain. I can't make
an impression on the rock."

The stranger answered with solemnity, "That isn't your

---

[1]Joseph P. Lash, *Helen and Teacher*. (New York: Delacorte Press,
1980), 52.

concern. Your duty is to pick, whether the rock breaks or not. The work is yours. The results are in other hands."

The minister went back to work. At the first stroke the rock shattered.

I often think of memorization that way. For some months now I have been working to memorize the book of Revelation. I've reached chapter ten now. But it's been hard going—more difficult than any other book I've ever done. I don't know why. But it seems that so many lunchtimes (when I do my memory work) I simply don't "feel" like laboring in the verses. I'll get stuck on a few verses. I simply can't get them into my head. Then just as suddenly, when I'm about to give up, there's a break, and in a few days I've done twenty verses at once.

I'm convinced Satan will do anything to keep a person from memorizing the Word. It's hard work, and at first it can appear to have few rewards. That's not true, but the greatest of all rewards comes with it—the knowledge that you have pleased your Lord.

The Benefits

What then are the rewards of Bible memory work? Let me detail ten.

1. *Knowing Scripture by heart enables you to meditate on the Word anywhere, any time.* David often spoke of meditating on God "in the night watches" (Ps. 63:6-8, NASB). I don't think he pored over a scroll at those moments. I'm certain he replayed in his mind words he'd long ago memorized, perhaps even composed himself.

One man I know likes to meditate while shaving. Another does it on his way to work. A woman friend makes time for meditation while jogging. They can meditate at those times because the Word is written on their hearts. Only rigorous memorization can do that.

2. *It enables us to know the triune God intimately.*
I've often wondered how other people think, what goes on
in their minds. But have you ever thought about how God
thinks, what goes on in His mind? You needn't speculate.
The Bible is His mind revealed. By knowing God's Word,
we literally know His own thoughts on every conceivable
subject.

3. *It's a key to walking in the Spirit.* Two passages
of Scripture are indelibly linked. The first is Ephesians
5:18-21, the passage about being filled with the Spirit. The
other is Colossians 3:16-17. Interestingly enough, both
passages refer to the same results of a certain action—
"speaking to one another in psalms and hymns and spiritual songs," and "giving thanks for all things." But the preceding actions in each section are different. In Ephesians,
it's "Do not get drunk with wine, for that is dissipation, but
be filled with the Spirit, speaking to one another ... "
(Eph. 5:18, NASB). In Colossians, Paul's dictum is, "Let the
Word of Christ richly dwell within you." (Col. 3:16, NASB).
Do you get the idea that being "filled with the Spirit" and
letting God's Word richly dwell within you could be the
same thing?

If that is true, then memorizing God's Word gives the
Spirit the power to lead, guide, challenge, and instruct us.
Like a maestro at the piano, He is enabled to play upon our
spirit and remind us of the truths of God in every situation
of the day.

Andrew Bonar spoke of a man who had "meditated
through the Bible three times." That's a far more indepth
discipline than simply reading it. Such discipline drenches
the disciple with the dew of heaven and empowers him or
her to walk in godliness.

4. *The Spirit can apply the Word to the situation.*
The key to applying God's Word is learning to apply it
according to its meaning and context. If you read the story

of the temptation of Jesus in the wilderness in Matthew 4:1-11, it's awe-inspiring to see Him quote Scripture to the devil. In each situation Jesus chose precisely the words that applied to His need and situation.

I once heard John MacArthur say, "whenever I think about sinning, the Spirit hits me with six verses against it. I can't just sin anymore and enjoy it. I know too much Scripture." People who sink deep roots in the Word are not blown over by gusts.

5. *The Spirit continually gives you insight into God, and the truths of Scripture.* When you memorize God's Word and know it by heart, you'll find that God speaks to you at the strangest moments. You'll be driving along thinking about nothing important, when suddenly the Spirit strikes. An insight about a verse or truth lodges in your mind. Instantly, there's a sense of joy and discovery that draws you closer to the Lord.

While working on a children's novel, I struggled with a character's question of why evil came into his life. I had many good answers. But suddenly I saw new light in the brief line, "Jesus wept' (John 11:35). When Lazarus died, Jesus didn't offer a theology of evil—He wept. It was a potent insight for me.

6. *Through it, He gives us depth in the truth.* Have you ever been in a debate with a Jehovah's Witness? Scary, huh? They seem to know so much Scripture. Some of us may be able to back up our beliefs with the Bible, but many cannot. It's memorization that gives us true depth. We not only know what we believe, but we know why.

On such doctrines as the deity of Christ, the inspiration of Scripture, the Trinity, and salvation, any Christian should be able to turn to five texts that illuminate our beliefs. But many can't even find one.

Phil Donahue had a TV show one weekday with several homosexuals. There were a number of Christians in the audience. During the question and answer time, the Christians argued with the homosexuals that the Bible condemned their behavior. The argument went back and forth for several minutes, each maintaining the Bible supported their position, with no agreement. Suddenly, Donahue stopped everything and said, "Okay, you say the Bible is against homosexuality, and you say it isn't. Each of you show me where in the Bible you get support for your position."

Everyone played dumb for a moment, then the gay party produced a Scripture that really said nothing about homosexuality. Donahue turned to the Christian contingent. Do you know that no one in that room of over a hundred could produce a single verse that supported their argument? It was a horrible shame for Christians. How can we ever expect anyone to honor our Lord's truth when we don't?

7. *The Spirit shows you the unity of a whole book.* If you memorize whole books of the Bible you'll find an amazing thing: you'll begin not only to understand the book better, but you'll begin to understand its unity, integrity, and depth. The Spirit will open your mind to the Scriptures in dramatic, illuminating ways.

As you memorize Scripture you'll see why an author said what he did where. You'll grasp his whole frame of mind and the background to his thoughts. You'll begin to see connections between books. It's an incredible mind-opening process.

8. *You begin to get the broad scope of theology.* As you memorize more and more, you'll begin to see how everything in Scripture connects. You'll dig right into the mind of God. You'll see how He thinks and why. You'll understand His heart.

As I studied the book of Jonah some time ago, I was amazed at the process of discipline revealed in the book. By the end of it, I saw one thing in graphic detail: God wanted Jonah, more than anything, to understand His heart. He wanted Jonah to see why He loved those people in Nineveh and why He didn't want to destroy them.

As I studied, it really hit me: the Bible is much more than a volume of stories and theology; it's the revelation of God's very heart. As you memorize you will be sinking your heart into His.

9. *You begin to see connections between passages.* You become a veritable walking concordance. You can connect all sorts of ideas through relating one verse you've memorized to another, especially if you begin memorizing whole books of Scripture. You become able to correlate truths and concepts, not just words.

10. *God gives you the capacity for more.* One thing I've always worried about in memorizing Scripture was reaching a saturation point. Would my mind reach a point where there was just too much? Would I begin to overflow, unable to retain more?

Yet, I've been memorizing for over seventeen years now and there's no stopping point in sight. In fact, my mind has become keener, more logical, more able to assimilate data than ever before.

It carries over into everything—my work, my home, my hobbies. The mind becomes sharper, more focused than ever.

The beauty of Bible memorization is that anyone, anywhere with the commitment can do it. You don't have to be a genius or a mental giant. But it is a question of discipline. You just have to decide that you'll do it. The question is, will you?

Five

YOU
CAN
MEMORIZE
BOOKS
OF THE
BIBLE

The one tool that I've found to be most useful in daily life is Scripture memorization. I find that one's capacity for memorizing the Bible only increases. As I mentioned earlier, it took me a whole week to get down my first verse in the winter of 1973. But now I can memorize a chapter in a week, if it's short enough and if I push myself. I have found knowing the Word in my heart to be energizing, challenging, and empowering. It's like having your own internal encyclopedia. Or like Spurgeon said, "Cut him anywhere and he bleeds Bibline"—the Bible.

The memorizer of Scripture will never be without guidance, encouragement, or wisdom. Often, Scriptures will come to mind that apply to situations—without even asking. When they are stored in the heart and the need arises, the Spirit pulls the truth out into view.

I'm convinced that not only is memorizing verses possible for any Christian, but that it's possible for many of us to memorize whole books of the Old and New Testaments. Hard to believe? It can be done. Islamic students are required to memorize the whole Koran for their ordination.

Why shouldn't Christians learn whole books moving toward the goal of memorizing the entire New Testament?

I've spent years thinking about and practicing Bible memorization. While in seminary I met Gary Friesen, a young doctoral student who showed me a system that took me off the Memory Pack and put me on the memory file. My own memorization program rocketed. While I had logged quite a few verses through the Memory Pack system (which I'll talk about in a moment), this new method enabled me to keep hundreds of verses "word-perfect" with only fifteen minutes review a day.

Memorizing Scripture is an important way to learn to use the Bible in all of life. Frequently we need to discern God's will in a matter. Memorized Scripture gives a reference point for finding and practicing the truth.

That's the reason I put so much stock in Bible memory work. It not only puts the Word of God at your fingertips, but etches it upon your heart. No one can take it away or confuse you with falsehood. When Jesus was tempted in the wilderness, He didn't say to Satan, "Hold it, let Me look that up in My concordance." Rather, He countered each temptation with the same response: "it is written" (Matt. 4:4,7,10). He knew precisely what God's Word said— because He'd memorized it.

But there is more. My doctoral friend also put another goal in mind—the idea of memorizing the New Testament. < Even though at the time it looked like a project for someone with a 175 IQ, plus a photographic memory, gradually other people began to encourage me and it's now a goal I'd like to achieve in my lifetime.

A Starting Point

So where do you start? Frankly, memorizing whole books of the New Testament should not be the starting point. It is

wiser to start your memory program with specific verses—
hordes of them, if you can—than to plow right in on the
Sermon on the Mount or the Book of Ephesians. Many of
life's difficulties can be tackled better through knowing a
smattering of texts than through slugging it out in the
Book of Romans. While there are many of us who have
gone through numerous memory programs, have stocked
away hundreds if not thousands of verses, and would profit
by working on whole books of the Bible at a time, you still
have to start somewhere. And that place is with single
verses from the Bible.

The challenge itself should motivate. But also the sheer
love for the Bible and its Author drives us to want to know
everything He said—in heart and by heart.

I have found in my own life that Bible memory work
carries with it a consuming hunger for more learning.
Why? I believe it's because of what we see happen in our
lives as a result of memorizing Scripture. Anyone who has
faithfully practiced the discipline could catalog numerous
benefits of Bible memory work. In my life I have seen the
Lord transform attitudes, overcome problems, and redirect
or end habits—simply through the consistent memorization and application of Scripture. Many times, I am in the
heat of the hottest spiritual struggles when the Spirit of
God reminds me of a verse memorized years ago. Suddenly, that verse takes on new meaning and practicality.

A friend told me recently how the Lord had brought a
verse to his mind that instructed him in the midst of trying
circumstances. He remarked, "Nearly every verse I've
memorized has been used at one time or another to help
me walk straight while everything was teetering."

Still, how can one begin memorizing the Bible with a
view to learning whole books of the New Testament? Let
me suggest a few brief principles.

1. *Start small.* Build up a backlog of verses. Learn

many single verses, perhaps over 2,000, before you attempt whole books. Digesting many bite-size chunks will prepare you for the large meal ahead.

2. *Start with smaller books.* I found that by beginning with such books as Ephesians, Philippians, and those of six chapters or less, that I was continually encouraged and never felt under the pile. We need to see progress. Completing one book in a month or two jets on to the next one with joy.

3. *Be willing to give it the time necessary.* The hard part is not new memorization, it's reviewing regularly what you've already put on the brain tapes. Much of my time to and from work (forty-five minutes each way), at lunch, and in the evenings before bed is spent in either review or new memorization work. Ask yourself: "What time during the day can I double up on or use to greater advantage?" A fast sandwich at lunch can give you time for a soul-filling meal of Scripture.

4. *Let the Spirit help you develop your own methods.* While we are all constantly tempted to thrust our discoveries on others, saying, "This is THE method," we must remember that the Spirit teaches each one of us individually (1 John 2:27). Depend on Him to help you step by step.

Memory Methods

Memory work is hard. I do not have a photographic memory, nor do most of you who will read this book. Thus, for some of us, it's a grind. I personally memorize by rote. I simply repeat the verse and its address (the reference where the verse is found) over and over in my mind until I get it down.

Still, there are many methods of memorizing Scripture, not just by rote. I've set a number of verses to music. This firmly rivets the verse to mind and even sets it to a joyous tune. Sometimes, when I have to read one of those verses in public, it's hard not to break into song.

There are numerous other devices which I'll talk about in chapter 12. But I've come to the conclusion that simple rote, line by line, word by word memory is the best. Interestingly enough, our minds seem to have an unlimited capacity for this. I thought that I'd sooner or later reach a point of diminishing returns. My mind would become so saturated that I just couldn't memorize any more. But scientists tell us we use less than 10 percent of our brain capacity in our lifetimes. God has given us an incredible gift in our minds. It is impossible to be so saturated that you can't learn one more verse, chapter, or book. You can always go further and higher. It's only a question of the will.

The Role Of Review

The critical element in memorizing Scripture is review. How can you retain what you've already memorized?

Many Christians memorized verses while in Sunday School, but because they didn't review, lost them. Going over and over the verses systematically and regularly is the key. If you can come up with a method that will enable you to keep going over the verses you know on a weekly or monthly basis, you will never lose them.

Several methods I picked up along the way from others, and some I developed on my own are helpful. It might be helpful to think of these as three stages in the memory process.

The Bible Memory Pack

Many Christians will be instantly familiar with this methodology. It's simply a small pack of cards similar to a business card wallet. You put the verses on the cards, keep them in the pack in your pocket, and pull them out to work on at appropriate times—while standing in lines, in the bathroom, traveling, etc. This is a beginning stage. Often while standing in line at the supermarket or store you can pull out the pack and go through the cards. Look at the address and review the verse in your mind, saying it to yourself. Then say the address again to fix it in place. Then move on to the next card. I found I could review thirty or forty verses while standing in the supermarket. You can even do this while driving. It only takes a glance down at your card to see the address. You can review the verse in your mind as you drive. (I wouldn't recommend this for learning new verses, though, when you have to keep looking at the card.)

In learning new verses, you simply repeat the address and verse over and over until you can say it without looking at the text. Once it's fixed firmly in your mind, go on to the next verse and put the one you've learned in with other review verses.

This method is very handy. You can carry it anywhere, and unless you have an aversion to people wondering what you're looking at, no one will be the wiser. You'll know hundreds of verses by heart and never lose them again.

If you memorize two verses a week you'll have over a hundred verses logged in a year. And if you keep at it, in ten years you'll have over a thousand verses. Imagine what the Spirit can do with that in your heart.

Where To Get Them

You can get these memory packs in Christian bookstores as well from several organizations. Campus Crusade, the Navigators, and the Billy Graham Evangelistic Association all have such materials available. But if you stick with it you'll soon run out of verses because most of these materials are limited. What I do is use business cards and write (or type) verses I like or need on the cards. As I read the Bible I'm always coming across a verse I like, so I put it on a card and memorize it.

The important thing is that once you begin doing this, you also keep reviewing the verses you've already learned, once a week at least.

How Can You Stick With It?

But how can you stick with it? Millions of Christians start off memorizing Scripture with gung ho but they often end up hung low. They give up. Why?

Remember that Satan and his cohorts will do anything to keep you from living a godly spiritual life. You're in a battle. Expect the devil to throw a fit if you take memorizing Scripture seriously. He'll heave everything he can at you—television, procrastination, tiredness, boredom, money problems, you name it. He'll use anything and everything to keep you from getting those verses down. But remember, "Greater is He who is in you than he who is in the world" (1 John 4:4), and He will see us through.

After you've logged enough verses to fill up the pack, you may want to try the next method to avoid carrying around a memory pack that looks like a suitcase.

The Bible Memory File

Once you've used the Bible memory pack for a lengthy period of time you'll be confronted with another problem besides the awkwardness of carrying it around: It becomes difficult to review all those verses and keep them organized.

I reached this point after about a year of memorizing

verses of my own and from the Campus Crusade "Bible Memory Pack." But then I met Garry Friesen on the Dallas Seminary campus. He offered some students the opportunity to enter into a discipleship methodology he'd learned as a young Christian. I jumped in and learned how to use what he called a "Bible Memory File."

This is a review system using 3" x 5" cards. I continued to use my Bible Memory Pack for learning new verses, because I could use it wherever I was during the day simply by pulling out the pack. But the file system helped me tremendously in setting up a systematic way for tracking and reviewing every verse I'd ever learned.

This is the way it works. Divide the file into three sections: "Daily review", "Weekly review", and "Monthly review." The "Daily file" contains all the verses that you are presently working on and need to review once a day (in conjunction with the Memory Pack). The "Weekly" file is divided into seven sections and contains verses you know well enough to review only once a week. They are labeled "Monday," "Tuesday," etc. and are reviewed only on the appropriate day of the week. The "Monthly" file has thirty sections and contains verses you know well enough to review only once a month.

I found that I could review up to sixty verses on any given day in about fifteen to twenty minutes with this file system.

How It Works

How then does it work? At the time that you would normally study the Bible and pray, you add a special memorization time as well. It only takes about ten to twenty minutes, depending on how many verses you have to review. So, say it's Monday, March 21. You simply pull out the "Daily," "Monday," and "21" files and review the verses on the cards in them. You might have five new verses in the "Daily" file, twelve in the "Monday" group, and thirty-two for day 21. You simply look at the address, then repeat the verse in your mind (or out loud, which is better) without looking at the actual words. Then you quickly read it over to make sure you got it right.

This provides a systematic method of reviewing verses on a regular basis. You don't have to worry about where and when you'll be going over each verse, because they're all in your file. I found this system enabled me to keep over 2,000 verses in near "word-perfect" shape.

If you find that you've lost a verse in your memory, you can always place it in a higher frequency file. Occasionally I'd discover that I couldn't repeat a verse in my monthly file. So I'd simply transfer it into the daily or weekly file and soon have it in word-perfect order again.

Sticking With It

It's important to remember again that Satan is not going to like this. Anyone committed enough to practice such a system will get dynamited daily. I don't mean that as a scare tactic. But he'll do anything to take that time away from you. So you have to guard that time with your life.

You also must guard against turning this discipline into a legalistic practice. That is, if you find yourself thinking, "Uh oh, I didn't do my verses today. I won't be able to live for God effectively" you're probably getting into a legalistic rut. If you miss, don't beat yourself about it. Pick it up the next day, or put in some extra time.

What matters is that you endure and not give up. I guarantee that if you hold the pattern for a few months, you'll never lose it. In my first ten years as a Christian I reached a point where I'd memorized over 2,500 verses. That was when I discovered a need to move on to another system.

The Whole Book Memory System

While using the Bible Memory File I realized I had so many verses memorized in a particular Bible book that it might be wise to learn the whole book. I decided simply to link up all the verses I already knew with the ones in-between.

This method became an overwhelmingly joyful process. For the first time I began to understand the scope and power of the Scriptures. Whole books came alive. I saw why the author said what he did in one place and why he didn't say something in another. My own spiritual life was deepened and broadened beyond all expectation.

When I began this stage the Holy Spirit seemed to lead me daily in an evolutionary process of development. He helped me learn as I went along. I have discovered now that on a six-week cycle I can review all the books I've been learning as well as delve into more. The beauty of the process is that all I need to do is carry around a small pocket Bible. No more memory packs or files for me, just the Scriptures which come in handy for unexpected counseling and witnessing opportunities.

What I do is simply review the book on the day and week listed. When I first started the chart looked like this:

DAY:	Mon.	Tues.	Wed.	Thurs.	Fri.
	Eph. 1	2	3	4	5

As I went on and learned more books of the Bible, it expanded to something like this:

DAY:	Mon.	Tues.	Wed.	Thurs.	Fri.
	Eph.	Gal.	Col.	Phil.	2 Tim.

As I continued on, I have expanded even more and find that I can simply keep on going without hindrance:

WK:	Mon.	Tues.	Wed.	Thurs.	Fri.
1.	Matt. 1–5 +2 John	Matt. 6–10 +3 John	Heb. 1–7	Rev. 1–8	Rev. 9–11 +Rom. 9–11
2.	Rom. 1–8	Gal.	Heb. 8–13		
3.	Eph.	Phil. + Jude	1 Cor. 1–8		
4.	Col.+ 2 Thes.	1 Thes.	1 Cor. 9–16		
5.	1 Tim.	2 Tim.	1 Peter		
6.	Titus+ 2 Peter	James	1 John		

Ultimately, I expect that I can put the whole New Testament into a review grid of a cycle of about six to eight weeks. That will mean I will be reviewing the whole New Testament by memory once every two months. That goal drives me diligently. Though it's still many years away, each new chapter memorized becomes a milestone along the way.

Take Note

But note several things about this arrangement. First, I am reviewing about six to ten chapters a day. This can usually be done in about sixty minutes. I usually do this during my drive to and from work (which is about forty-five minutes each way). I can review the books in my mind (or out loud) while driving, without destroying my concentration on the road. It's really no different from listening to the radio or a tape, except the tape is playing back in *my* mind.

The beauty of this is that often the Spirit gives me time to meditate on these Scriptures as I go through them. Wisdom, insight, and understanding become a present reality.

It's important though that you also read through these memorized books at times to make sure you're not making substitutions and changing God's Word. Thus, I also have a system of reading the same chapters I reviewed sometime during that day. This helps rivet it further in my mind. I usually do this during breaks in the day or at night. The important thing is that you not only review the books by memory, but have a system for making sure what you're reviewing is correct. I've found that it's easy to get a certain phrase in mind that's not a correct reading of the verse. Through reading over the passages you've reviewed, you're able to catch those mistakes and correct them.

There are some mornings, however, when I feel nearly dead and my mind can't concentrate. That's only human. On such mornings, I do as much as I can and hope the next day will be better.

Second, notice on my outline that Thursdays and Fridays are spent reviewing the same books each week. These are books I've recently memorized. They need more work than others, so I put them in these slots to review them once a week, instead of once every four weeks. It's important when I first memorize a book that I nail it down deep in my heart. That weekly review is important in getting the words fixed for good.

Third, the cycle can easily be expanded to more weeks as newly memorized books are added.

Fourth, the weekends can be used as "catch-up" times.

Obviously, this is a method that suits me. Anyone could use it, but it is always best to let the Spirit teach you your own innovations as you go along. No human method can take the place of His leading.

New Material

How then do you get new material down? Each day at work
I have an hour lunch break. At that time I take a walk
through the neighborhood and work on new passages. I
simply go through the verses rote, repeating them one by
one until I have down a whole chapter. If I take thirty
minutes for this (the other thirty is for prayer), I can usually get through one to four new verses. At the same time, I
review the verses in the chapter memorized up to the point
each day so that I don't lose them.

The key is to make time for this new material. Carve a
niche in your day. This is what I do. I'm no genius. I'm not
in full-time ministry. But I believe anyone who wants to do
it can—with God's power and blessing.

A Matter Of The Heart

Bible memorization is a matter of the heart. No one can
stick with it whose heart isn't committed to it. It's something we do out of love for the Lord, not because of pres-
sure from a tradition, pastor, or group. Thus, what I have
provided here is only a pointer. You can use it and develop
it as the Spirit teaches you.

But frankly, I'm excited. The idea of memorizing the
New Testament started with me over ten years ago as an
"impossible dream." It still seems a long way down the
road. Whether any of us ever actually memorizes the New
Testament "word-perfect" isn't really the point. Many
Pharisees probably memorized much of the Old Testament
and Jesus called them vipers and white-washed tombs. It's
the Scriptural truth we're applying and practicing that
counts. And it's this process of learning new truths and
applying them day by day that Jesus applauds.

Six

MINING
FOR
TREASURE

There are many different kinds of ice cream. Frankly, I like most of them. But there's one kind I enjoy more than any of the others. It's called "Ben and Jerry's Heath Bar Crunch." Ben and Jerry are two Vermont men who some years ago recognized there was a distinct problem in the ice cream industry. All the ice creams on the market featured nice flavors, but when it came to any that had something in it—like chocolate chips, nuts, cherries, or raisins—they noticed that most makers chopped the pieces up into such teeny bits that you could barely taste them.

Ben and Jerry set out to rectify the situation. Their ice cream would have chunks—little icebergs of flavor. Now Heath Bar Crunch is just that. Ever had a Heath Bar? Ben and Jerry crush them up into pieces anywhere from a quarter inch to two inches long! When you bite into one of them, your mouth knows it and momentarily whooshes off into Heath Bar heaven. I try not to eat too much of it, but when I do it's always a marvelous journey into the bliss of ice cream hedonism.

What does that have to do with Bible study? Just this,

there are too many of us groping around for one lick of
those little bitty specks of chocolate in our Usual Kind
Brand Ice Cream when in reality Ben and Jerry's
Superchunk is always available. Bible study can be a
source of the greatest joy in life—if we'd just give it the
right amount of time and effort, and the proper approach.
And it's through such Bible study that we can learn to use
the Scriptures in all of life.

So Many Methods

When I first began to study the Scriptures, I just read and
studied them as though they were a special love note from
God to me. I don't know how I happened upon that methodology, but I was convinced that the Lord Jesus spoke
directly to me through His Word.

Then I found out there were many special ways to study
the Bible. There was the inductive method, the topical
method, the historical/cultural/grammatical approach, the
five-minute hipshot, the fifteen-minute deeper dive, the
thirty-minute sink till you swim, the four-hour grind
through the mind, and the fifteen-hour straight once-in-a-
lifetime hurtle-directly-into-heaven kind for the
superscholars. Frankly, I found myself getting confused
and upset. To my mind, some of these so-called methods
were turning my Bible study into a dry bones, analytical
crawl through a desert, rather than a meeting with the Lord
of the universe and a chance to listen to Him.

But as I worked away at it, I found that just as there's a
balance in most areas of life, there's one in Bible study. No
method is always right; some are definitely wrong (the
allegorical one—looking for the symbolic meaning in everything regardless of the author's original intent—for instance). It's best to learn to take a variety of approaches
until it becomes second nature.

Sometimes simply reading the Bible like a good story is fine. At other times, you might want to trace through a single word or expression. In still others, the grammatical construction will yield life-transforming data. It's a matter of practice, familiarity, and personal growth. In-depth, scholarly analysis can be as much a tryst with the Lord as seeing a dramatic reading of the Sermon on the Mount. In fact, I had a friend in seminary who read a Greek grammar one year as part of his quiet time!

Mining Treasure

But how do you get to the point of discovering spiritual treasure as you study? That is, how do you gain insight through the Scriptures that not only instructs but ignites you.

I guess we have to remember that our goal here isn't some mystical pleasure, but a walk and talk with the Lord. At times His words will convict; we'll come away saddened and repentant, bent on change. At other times, His words will break our moping and lift us up onto a cloud of hope. Still other times, He will reveal to us new truths about Himself that will cut across all our long-held ideas. He could throw us into a spiritual tailspin on purpose—to bring us back into line with truth. I find that Bible study frequently shatters my illusions about God and His Kingdom.

The Nine Principles

Let me offer you nine principles to move you in the direction of mining the Scripture's treasure. Remember though, these only work when applied diligently and consistently. You can't expect to pick up the Bible one day and instantly land on insights Luther and Calvin only dreamed of. Nor should you approach it with the attitude that you'll be jolted out of your socks every time you open the Book. There will be dry times too.

Like The Newspaper

The first principle is to read the Bible like you would the daily newspaper or any other book. That's not to say that you don't recognize it's a Word from God and therefore demands utter reverence and obedience unlike other literature. But the Bible was written to be read normally, the way language normally works. It's to be taken at face value, like a newspaper reports the facts in common terms. We don't need to think there's some hidden deeper meaning in everything that's said.

Computer people refer to something called WYSIWYG — or *wizziwig* —which means, "What you see is what you get." That is, what's on the computer screen will come out the same way on the printer.

In some ways that's a good hermeneutical approach to the Bible. "What it says is what it means" unless it's obvious from the context and for other reasons (which we'll discuss in the next chapter) that something else is meant. That means you understand the words of the Bible plainly, simply, literally, normally. Don't attach some outlandish idea to it.

This is the theological error that most cults fall prey to. They often focus on insignificant issues and in so doing "major on the minors" at the expense of Christ. Strange as it may seem, there are plenty of people who use the Bible in this way, stretching the words to prove the most incredible meaning they can draw out of it.

Avoid such mistakes, read the Bible like you would any other book. You'll not only find it enjoyable, but easy to understand as well.

The Right Version

Second, choose a Bible translation which is easy to understand. I personally like to use the *New American Standard*, largely because that was the first Bible I used as a Christian and later the source for the verses I memorize. There are plenty of excellent versions available. The *New International Version* may soon become the standard of our day. But there is also the *New King James*, the *Berkeley*, the *Revised Standard*, as well as the traditional *King James*.

The important thing in choosing a study Bible is to find one you can easily read and understand. That's part of the problem for many younger people with the *King James*. The English is archaic and when they read it, they simply don't understand. The purpose of a study Bible is to facilitate understanding, not hamper it.

By study Bible I simply mean the one you will primarily use for study. It should be an accurate and accepted translation that gets as close to the Lord's original intent as possible. Others—paraphrases like *The Living Bible*, *Good News Bible*, and *The Amplified Version*—are not study Bibles in the same sense. They interpret for you and bring their own biases and theological persuasions into the text. A good study Bible should avoid that problem.

Choosing the best version for you is an important decision. Sometimes it's best to choose the same one your pastor or church uses. You might want to go to a Christian bookstore and ask to see several. Then read a few familiar passages in each Bible to see how they are treated. Try something from the Old Testament, and in the New Testament something from the Gospels, the epistles, and Revelation. See how it flows and sings, then make your choice. Remember, whatever one you choose may be with you for many years, so choose carefully.

Learn To Make Observations

The third principle involves the process of observation. When I was a student at Dallas Theological Seminary, one of the first courses we took was called "Inductive Bible Study." The first step of that process was called observation. We were given an assignment—to make twenty-five observations about one verse in Scripture, Acts 1:8. The teacher gave us direction about how to make observations and we went at it. It was hard going. The first ten were easy. But eleven through twenty-five only came with sweat. I bounded into class the next day sure I'd discovered something no one in all of history had noticed.

The professor didn't even give us a chance to catch our breath. Next assignment: make twenty-five more observations. Everyone groaned. But we came back with our fifty thoughts.

Then in class we began combing through the text. Students shared their insights. I was astonished. I found myself staring at the verse, saying to myself, "How come I didn't see that?" When we were done, the teacher had over 100 different insightful observations written down on overheads. How could one get so much out of one verse?

The answer is simple: observe. Take a look. Write down what you see. Envision yourself as a private investigator deciphering every shred of fact and fiction to solve a case. Look at words, grammar, things, places, persons. You might discover allusions to other truths, a quotation from another text, a comparison to something in another passage or even a book. Comb through those texts. Pull out everything. Leave no word, no phrase, no idea unturned.

What's most invigorating about this process is that when you write it all down you soon find that one observation leads to others. For instance, I got into Psalm 23 one day and started writing down ideas. "The Lord is my shepherd" (v. 1). I began asking questions. Who is this Lord? What does the word *Lord* mean? Why does David use the word *Lord* instead of God, or Almighty, or Father? How does "is" come into it? Was David aware of a presence? Why "shepherd"? What is the significance of "my"? If He's my shepherd, that means I'm His sheep. What is the significance of that? How am I like a sheep? How is a sheep like me?

As I answered those questions through my observations it seemed that the text came alive in a multitude of ways. Then I rooted deeper. Where was David when he wrote this? Was he young or old, and what would be the significance of his age? Why did David write this Psalm? Who was he writing for and why? I asked all the who, what, where, when, how, and why questions I could. Then I got into "wherefore." What did it all have to do with me?

It seemed as I bombarded the text and the rest of the Bible with my questions, my joy and interest mounted. I felt as though I was winging along on a wave of spiritual power. As you learn to observe whenever you read the Bible, things begin to come alive in a powerful way. You feel as though you're right there with the writer, delivering the lines yourself to an expectant crowd.

Visualize

That leads to a fourth thought. Learn to visualize what is happening in a text. This works best with historical situations, but you can also do it with anything in the Bible.

What is it to visualize? Get yourself into the situation. Use your imagination to begin seeing what was happening, what the people looked like, the tone of voice, everything you can think of. See it like a movie in your mind — a movie in which you can get into the minds and hearts of the people involved.

There's a danger here of course. You don't want to read into the text things that aren't there. But on the other hand, to sink down deep into a situation you have to picture something in your mind. In a way, we have to trust the Spirit to lead us. If we get off into farfetched nonsense, we can always ask Him to alert us to our heresy. But on the other hand, no one can read the Gospels without getting some kind of mental image of New Testament times.

How then do you do this? Take a story like the one in Mark 3 where Jesus healed the man with the withered hand. As you go through the action, start to see what was happening. There's a crowd there, and Jesus, and then this man with the withered hand. What does the man look like? What's he feeling? Is he used to being in this situation? Is he the kind of guy who jumps into the action, or do you see him as someone on the sidelines, perhaps hidden a bit from the main scenery? Is he young or old?

These are the types of questions to ask. You see this can go on and on. Of course, many of the details we're talking about here are not revealed in the Bible. But that really doesn't matter. We should base our principles and theology only on what is revealed. But we can use our redeemed imaginations to put a little fire and drama into the situation to see it more clearly. It has a way of making the truth jump off the page.

Carve Out A Block Of Time

A fifth application relates to the time you spend in the Word. While quick reads and short dives into the text are nice, there's a place for some in-depth study too. If you can find the time to watch twenty-six hours of television a week (as the average American does), then you can carve out a special period of two or three hours when you give Him and His Word your undivided attention. That means mining with real tools—a Bible dictionary, concordance, atlas, and commentary. It means getting at the root of words, finding out their meanings, and toiling in the text like a detective in search of clues. You might even try to incorporate such study in conjunction with a class you're taking or teaching.

This kind of practice should become part of our regular spiritual lives. At one time I found the idea of studying for several hours straight a reason for terror. I likened it to running up a mountain in full sprint. I thought, "What would I do with all that time?"

Having logged many hours and days over the years in such study, I can only say it pays rich dividends, far beyond anything we can get in simple reading. There is something joyous in unearthing a truth, drawing it out into the light of day, and gazing at it under the microscope of spiritual insight.

The two disciples whom Jesus met on the road to Emmaus after His resurrection had an experience that illuminates what real study can do. After Jesus taught them the truths about Himself and disappeared, they said, "Were not our hearts burning within us while He talked with us on the road and opened the Scriptures to us?" (Luke 24:32)

"Our hearts burning within us!" That's the experience we're after. That's the meeting of God, truth, and human spirit. There's a burning, a scouring away that reveals the solid silver of faith, hope, and love.

It can be any Christian's experience as he or she toils in the Word. But it takes commitment and desire to be *delighted by discipline*.

Develop A Habit

A sixth principle concerns the habit of Bible intake. There are a multitude of ways to imbibe the Word. The important

fact is, though, that you do it regularly and consistently. As
Peter said, "Like newborn babes, crave pure spiritual milk
(1 Peter 2:2). My wife has just had our second child. I'm
amazed at all I'd forgotten about it—the waking at all
hours of the night to feed the baby, the insistent crying,
the demand for "milk, more milk, more milk, now—or I'll
keep you up all night!" That kid wants it constantly! And
that's the way it should be for Christians too.

There are plenty of positive habits that should be a part
of our lives. But the one we can't survive without is the
daily intake of the Word of God. When I neglect my reading, study, and memorization habits, I find there's a boredom with life, an itchiness and restlessness that won't go
away. Using the Bible in all of life means making it a habit-
ual pattern, part of your everyday routine.

Ask God

Seventh, remember that whenever you approach the Bible,
you have its Author right there inside you. Ask Him questions. If a problem throws you, or there appears to be a
contradiction to some other truth you know about, or you
just can't grasp a concept—lay it at His feet. John told his
readers that we have an "anointing"—the Spirit of God
residing within us, who is able to teach us (1 John 2:27).
He may not reveal the answer today or tomorrow, but He
will eventually. It may not hit you till five years from now,
but I've found that He does answer all our questions.

Pascal said, "All the evils of life have fallen upon us
because men will not sit quietly in a room." I might add
"and pray."

During a time of trial, I repeatedly cried out to God,
"Why is this happening to me?" My roommate responded,
"You can't ask God *why*. He won't answer. Ask him *what*
to do."

That became a potent answer to prayer. God had given me insight through my friend.

That's the real joy of Christianity. We're not out here on our own. Our Lord goes with us and ahead of us every step of the road.

Try Some Creative Approaches

The next principle is to learn to use your creativity. There are many ways you can approach Bible study. Irving Jensen of Bryan College has built a reputation on his ability to make charts of books, chapters, and even paragraphs and verses of the Bible. His Moody Press Bible Study Guides are excellent and helpful.

Walk Thru the Bible Ministries also offers numerous creative approaches to the Bible through devotionals, charts, and catchy slogans and phrases that help people learn the greatest Book of the ages.

This kind of creativity is latent in all of us, and, if tapped, can become a source of deep insight and joy. I'd encourage you to read books on Bible study, try different methods, and practice them in your quiet time, teaching, and personal work. If you keep in mind that Bible study is work that will yield high dividends in the process, you will win.

Share It

The final principle for study is this: share what you're learning. Tell someone—not to impress them, but simply as an encouragement and exhortation to delve into the Scriptures. True Bible study will not produce anything less than humility. The humble person has a way of giving that carries a flavor of love and even altruism.

One of my favorite people is a young man name Doug

White. Every now and then we get together for breakfast or a family outing. Doug is always bubbling over with some new truth or idea he's discovered. We love to sit down over coffee and debate, discuss Scripture, play devil's advocate, and challenge one another. Talking with him is always an exhilarating time because I know he'll have something interesting to offer.

In fact, that's one of the great benefits of consistent Bible study—there's always something new to share, some insight you've crabbed out of the harbor that needs just a little boiling and seasoning.

I like what Dr. Howard Hendricks used to tell his students when they'd give him some new observation about a verse. He told us, "I shout, froth at the mouth, and fairly need to be led away."

I think a little of that can happen to the student of the Word who will feed regularly on a "stuff-yourself-to-the-gills" diet of the Bible. You will get to the point where you not only see God in everything, but you can't see anything but God wherever you go!

Seven

IS
WHAT
I THINK
IT SAID
WHAT
IT SAID?

There's an old story about a fellow who believed in a Bible study practice called "verse-dipping." He'd pray about a problem, then flip open his Bible, plunk his finger down on a verse, and believe that was the Spirit's answer to his problem.

He followed this process in resolving a severe problem he was having, opened the text, and plunked down on Matthew 27:5: "He [Judas] went away and hanged himself."

That didn't sound like the best answer to his problem, so he flipped again. This time he landed in Luke 10:37: "Go and do likewise."

He was getting nervous about this, but decided to give it one more try. He breathed out a prayer, flipped the pages, and his fingertip alighted on John 13:27: "What you are about to do, do quickly."

The apocryphal story is humorous, but it is not without its message. It points out the problem of biblical interpretation. The wrong approach and the faulty interpretation can lead to disaster. I understand that the Ku Klux Klan bases some of their beliefs on the Bible. So do the Jehovah's Witnesses, Christian Scientists, and Scientologists. How you interpret what the Bible says is critical to your successful use of it in everyday life.

What Does It Mean?

When you seek to interpret Scripture, you must ask a simple question: "What does it mean?"

There are some people who will say in this regard, "You can use the Bible to prove anything." Yes, if you push it, stretch it, and read between the lines in ways the Bible doesn't sanction, you could use it to justify many wrong things. But you could just as well do that with the Declaration of Independence, Reader's Digest, or a recipe for Kentucky Fried Chicken. If you're going to dismiss all the laws of language and meaning and "do your own thing," then who cares about interpretation anyway?

But when it comes to language and the science of interpretation (which is called hermeneutics), there are some specific and simple rules to follow in making the right interpretation. And if there's any book we want to interpret rightly, it's the Bible.

For anyone interested in an in-depth study of the science of biblical interpretation, I recommend Bernard Ramm's *Protestant Biblical Interpretation* (Baker Book House, 1970) or R.C. Sproul's *Knowing Scripture* (InterVarsity Press, 1977). My purpose here is simply to give you some basic guidelines for understanding what you're reading in the Bible.

At The Start

In beginning any kind of Bible study, you must determine several important facts. *First, what kind of literature are*

you dealing with? The Bible contains many different liter-
ary forms, from simple history to poetry, prophecy, proverbs, parables, doctrine, and drama. To interpret correctly,
you have to be sure what you're working with.

For instance, many people take the Proverbs as promises about how life will operate for them. They believe that
Proverbs 22:6 which says, "Train a child in the way he
should go, and when he is old he will not turn from it,"
guarantees that God will make their children turn out right.

But the Proverbs are not unconditional promises of God;
they're general observations about life. They speak of what
normally happens, not what will always happen.

Similarly, someone might take the statement of Revelation 13:18 about the beast's number being 666. Years ago,
when Henry Kissinger was Secretary of State and making
news daily on his peace missions in the Mideast and Vietnam, someone discovered that if you transliterate "Henry
Kissinger" into Hebrew and give a numerical value to each
letter, you come up with 666. Therefore, he was the Anti-
christ. I'm sure the same thing could be done with President George Bush, Soviet leader Mikhail Gorbachev, and
Prime Minister Margaret Thatcher of Britain. This isn't true
biblical interpretation, but a stab at sensationalism.

*Second, we interpret Scripture in its grammatical
and historical context.* We should try to discover what
was being said in the original cultural, historical, and
grammatical situation. Whether we're looking at Paul's discussion of women wearing veils in 1 Corinthians 11, or at
the Last Supper scenes at the end of each of the Gospels,
we need to understand the culture, history, and grammar
employed. That wearing a veil was typical of that culture
had a lot to do with Paul's meaning for the Corinthians.
Similarly, knowing that people ate at a low table by lying
around it explains a lot about the conversations in the
Upper Room.

Whenever we read a passage of Scripture, we must always ask, "What did this mean in that time of life?" And, "What did the author mean in the context of his readers' situations?"

Third, what do other passages of Scripture say about this interpretation? If we discover some teaching that seems new and different, we need to find out if the same idea is taught elsewhere in the Bible. If God is indeed the Author of Scripture, and if He spoke from one mind and heart throughout history, then the Bible should be unified. There are no inherent contradictions. (There may be "apparent" ones, but they may be explained.) We can trust that the same truth will be revealed in other times and places, not just in one verse of Holy Writ. This means that if we can interpret a verse one of several ways, but only one is in harmony with the rest of Scripture, then that is the one we should choose. Our maxim should be *let Scripture interpret Scripture.*

For instance, the Mormons have a whole theology built on a single verse from 1 Corinthians 15:29 where Paul speaks of people being "baptized for the dead." Mormon theology interprets this to mean that a dead person who never believed can somehow be baptized and "saved" by a live believer being baptized in one's place.

The problem here is that nowhere else in Scripture do we find such a teaching. However, there is plenty of teaching on baptism. To interpret correctly (and this is an extremely hard verse), we should study the whole doctrine of baptism and then come to a conclusion about what possibilities there are on the basis of the whole Bible.

Finally, we must always remember that none of us is right all the time in our interpretations. Peter wrote, "No prophecy of Scripture came about by the prophet's own interpretation. For prophecy never had its origin in the will of man, but men spoke from God as they were carried along by the Holy Spirit" (2 Peter 1:20-21).

I have always wondered how two people who are filled with the Spirit and committed to Jesus Christ can come up with such diverse interpretations of the Word of God. I was horrified as a new Christian to learn that there were godly people on different sides of such issues as baptism, pre-destination, speaking in tongues, the millennium, and a multitude of other doctrines. As I studied, it seemed that no one agreed about anything! How can this be if we all believe in the same Lord and have the same Spirit?

Simply because we're all sinners, none of us is capable of being right about everything. The only one who was right about everything was Jesus. There's always room for growth, change, and admission of error.

If this is not so, then how is it that a Christian can change his mind about a doctrine at different times in his life? At one time I believed in infant baptism. I don't any longer. Which of me was right? At one time I believed God wasn't sovereign in the area of human salvation; now I do. Which Mark Littleton is correct?

Ultimately, we all have to proceed by faith, make our choices, and rely on the Spirit of God to lead and correct us when necessary. That's the essence of what it means to be Christian—none of us is perfect now, but we will be some day.

A Basic Tool

But is there some tool we can use to interpret correctly? Let me give you a short alliterated outline that I have found helpful. When you interpret the Bible, consider:

■ CONTENT. The actual words of the passage. What is said? What is not said? Beware of reading into it (eis-egesis); rather read out (exegesis) of it what is actual-ly there.

- CONTEXT. What is the context of the statement? How does it fit in to what has gone before and after?
- CULTURAL AND HISTORICAL BACKGROUND. Who is the author? What is his situation? What is the situation he is writing to? Find out all you can about the author, date, culture, and history of the passage.
- COMPARISON OF OTHER SCRIPTURES. What do other Scriptures say in relation to this passage? Are there any that have direct, or even indirect bearing to shed some light on it?
- COMMENTS OF OTHER PEOPLE. What have others said about this passage? This means reading commentaries (old and new) as well as listening to teaching tapes on the same verses.

Using this alliterated outline will help you follow the process of interpretation so that you're accurate and complete in your study.

Talk Through The Text

There are some creative things you can do that will aid biblical interpretation. Let me suggest several. One thing that can be done in Bible study is to learn to "talk through" a text. Read it and then talk it through, paraphrasing it like you would to a child. When you talk through the passage you have to put what's being said into your own words. Inevitably, you'll understand it better just by talking out loud to yourself.

Recently, I was struggling with the Book of Galatians. There were some statements in chapter 3 that utterly threw me. I couldn't figure out what they meant. Then I decided to talk through the whole book. I imagined myself reading the letter to that Galatian congregation and as I read, I explained what Paul meant. I paraphrased. As I listened to my voice and my mind trying to unify Paul's words, the book became more alive in my mind than ever. I suddenly saw the passion of Paul as he labored to persuade these people not to go back to living under the Law. I could feel him marshaling all his persuasive powers to make them understand. As I read and paraphrased Paul's words, I could feel new fire, similar to the fire Paul must have felt when he wrote them. It was an unforgettable experience.

Mull It Over

A second habit to get into is meditation. Take a passage and chew it over and over in your mind, playing it back like a tape until it is recorded in your heart. I'm going to explore this topic in-depth in chapter 8, but for now consider meditation as the lost art of true study. As you look through the Psalms, especially Psalms 119 and 63 you see what the psalmist did in the "night watches," spending time thinking about God's words and deeds.

Meditation is the most critical and also the most neglected element of Bible study for many Christians. Yet, it is the one thing you can do nearly anywhere, anytime. And it yields terrific benefits (which we'll look at later).

For now, practice the art of meditation by going over and over a passage in your mind, asking it questions, making observations, just thinking about it. Biblical meditation is not mystical, or superspiritual, or even esoteric. It's nothing akin to demonic practices like TM or Zen. Rather, it's a potent mental exercise that deepens understanding, fosters intimacy with God, and opens up new vistas to the heart and soul. It's loving God with all your mind.

Make Analogies

A third creative approach is the practice of making analogies and using illustrations to explain a truth to yourself.

When you study the Bible, train yourself to think in terms of—"How would I teach this truth to a six-year-old, or a teenager?"

Take a text like Romans 6:23, which many people know by heart. "For the wages of sin is death, but the gift of God is eternal life in Christ Jesus our Lord." In order to understand it better, think of an illustration that might explain "the wages of sin," "the gift of God," or "eternal life." You can go in any number of directions. For the "wages of sin," you might see an analogy to getting paid for work rendered. Or to a criminal getting sentenced to prison. Or the recompense you received when you did something wrong as a child.

A "gift" conjures up pictures of a birthday party, or Christmas. It's free. Undeserved. What kinds of examples can you think of for such a gift?

As I write this I am reminded of a story I read about a little boy in Vietnam during the war. A village was attacked and many children were killed and wounded. One little girl needed blood to survive. Since the medics involved couldn't speak much Vietnamese, they tried to make the children understand they needed blood to help this little girl live. Would any of the children give blood?

One little boy's hand went up hesitantly, then down, then up again, down. Finally he kept it up. His face was nearly white.

The nurses set up to take the blood and laid both the boy and the stricken girl down. But as they were taking the blood the little boy began crying and sniffling. No one knew what was wrong.

Finally, a Vietnamese woman came along who also spoke English. She talked with the little boy, trying to find out why he was crying. It was remarkable. The boy thought he was going to give all his blood to help the little girl. And he knew that he would die in the process.

Everyone was astonished. This boy had agreed, in a sense, to give his life that the little girl might live.

Someone finally asked him why he had agreed to do this. He quietly said, "She is my friend."

What a story! Yet, how perfect it speaks to the picture of a "free gift," and the sacrifice Jesus made on the Cross.

The point is clear. Through creating an analogy or discovering an illustration you will force yourself to grasp the text more clearly. Taking something abstract and putting it into the concrete through the use of a solid illustration always helps.

Good preachers do this all the time in their sermons. After making an abstract point or unfolding a principle, they try to illustrate it with an anecdote, story, comparison, or something from contemporary life. Suddenly the analogy sheds light on the principle.

When I taught a class of fourth through sixth graders, one of the lessons was on Philippians 2:5-8, which speaks of how Jesus "emptied Himself" (v. 7, NASB) of all rights as God and came among us as a servant. I wondered how I was going to present this truth to a group of upper elementary students. I ranged over a number of possibilities, but after some thought I decided on John 13 where Jesus washed the disciples' feet. But what was an apt analogy to Jesus' emptying Himself, yet at the same time being God incarnate? After some more thought, I imagined a high-ranking commanding officer going into the bunkhouse of a bunch of privates and washing their feet without them knowing who he was. In the end, he reveals himself as a general and everyone marvels.

That was when I hit paydirt. I borrowed a captain's uniform from a local student, put it on with all its shiny medals, then put a raincoat on over it. After that, I came into class and washed one of the kids' feet. That was astonishing enough to them. But when I took off the raincoat, they were all shocked. Why would an Army captain wash a fourth-grader's feet? Then I asked them, "Why would God come down and die for us?"

I don't know how much those kids understood, but it illuminated that passage in an unforgettable way for me.

Dear Friends

A fourth way to gain a greater understanding of a text is to write out an explanation of what it means as though you were writing to a friend. I have found that nothing clarifies one's thinking like having to write it out in a book, article, or letter. You can't be vague, speak in generalities, or pretend you know what you're talking about. Often the greatest writers are those who can communicate the truth in the simplest way. Why? Because to be able to simplify and make a truth comprehensible, you must first understand it yourself.

That's one reason I find writing so fascinating and fulfilling. I have learned that I've never truly studied until I've tried to explain it on paper to someone else. As I take notes, study, work through a truth, and come up with analogies, I find that to begin writing it down I inevitably have to work to grasp it more clearly. Often my first inclination and first thoughts aren't the best. So I dig deeper—mentally as well as into other texts—and come up with something even better. In fact, I'm convinced that in the "brainstorming" process the easiest ideas always come first. It's only when you go beyond the obvious that you strike the mother lode of truth that's there for the taking.

A Helpful Verse

There is much more that could be said about the process of biblical interpretation. But my purpose is merely to give you some guidelines so that you can use the Bible in your daily life. The Bible is not an easy book, but with the right sources and help, it can be understood.

One of Paul's exhortations to Timothy is helpful here: "Do your best to present yourself to God as one approved, a workman who does not need to be ashamed and who correctly handles the word of truth" (2 Tim. 2:15). There are six thoughts here that will guide anyone who earnestly seeks to know what the Bible says.

"Do your best." The word means to "be diligent." Give it all you got. Pour yourself into it.

"Seek to please God." As Paul says, "present yourself to God as one approved." God's approval is paramount. But how do you know when you've pleased Him? It's an intangible—perhaps something mystical. Paul wrote that the Spirit "testifies with our spirit" that we are God's children (Rom. 8:16), so there's also the reality of His "still small voice" speaking to our hearts and assuring us that we are pleasing Him. I'm not sure how it can be gauged, but I know I've experienced it. There's a freedom, liveliness, and exhilaration present when you're walking in the Spirit. This is not to be confused with a purely emotional experience or high. Rather, it's a deep-seated sense of peace, one "which passes all understanding" (Phil. 4:6-7, RSV). Paul knew when he was pleasing God and when he wasn't (see 1 Cor. 4:1-4). It's one of those elements of Christian living which can't be easily explained, but can be experienced.

"A workman." This literally means a laborer, one who works with his hands, a tradesman. Workers who don't produce a viable product soon go out of business. The Christian who handles Scripture facetiously or carelessly will soon find himself on the sidelines of spiritual life. If you're committed to Jesus' Word, then treat it with the highest respect and give it the best part of your workday.

"Who does not need to be ashamed." Did you ever get

caught staking your study and intelligence on some truth and then find out you were wrong? It can be considerably embarrassing. Think how the Pharisees must have felt when they confronted Jesus about some doctrine and Jesus replied, "Haven't you read?" (Matt. 12:3) No one likes to be caught in an error. Make sure when you study to do it thoroughly, so you can find backing for your beliefs.

"Correctly handles." Some translations have "rightly dividing." It's a word that means to cut a road in a straight direction, so that a traveler could go directly to his destination without making unnecessary detours. I once heard a well-known preacher say that he worked for three things in his preaching: clarity, accuracy, and practicality. That middle one is often the toughest. It's easy to let biases, preconceived notions, and other prejudices influence us. Be open to the truth, be accurate, and be committed to getting it right, even if it means a major change in your beliefs or outlook.

"The word of truth." Finally, remember that you're dealing with truth. Truth is a powerful tool. It can give life and hope, restrain sin, turn a person around, and open blind eyes.

Nothing was more terrifying a few years ago than when someone began tainting Tylenol bottles with poisoned pills. Several people died as a result and eventually a whole industry had to find a new way of packaging its product. Something we trusted suddenly became untrustworthy.

The Bible is truth, truth that will affect people's lives for all eternity. We can't be glib with it—in our own lives, or in the lives of others. If we want to use the Bible in all of life, we must be sure that we're applying it correctly and accurately. Otherwise we may poison our own lives as well as others.

Thomas Edison was once asked by a farmer if he knew of a way to kill potato bugs. The farmer had twenty acres and many of the vines were being destroyed. Edison tried numerous chemicals on the bugs. Bisulphide of carbon worked. Edison then bought a drum of it and went to the farm to sprinkle it on the vines. All the bugs dropped dead.

But the next day the farmer called excitedly and said his vines had died the previous night. Edison was caught. The inventor ended up paying $300 (at that time a high sum) because he had failed to experiment properly.

Study of the Bible is like that experimentation. Faulty observation and interpretation of the facts leads to faulty application. Come to the Word humbly, knowing that it contains life. Come to it hopefully, realizing that it can transform your own life. But above all, come to it respectfully, knowing that He who wrote it will call you to account for how you responded to it.

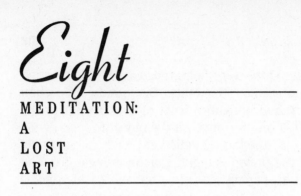

Eight

MEDITATION: A LOST ART

Merely memorizing and studying God's Word is not enough. As the Apostle Paul warned, "Knowledge puffs up . . . The man who thinks he knows something does not yet know as he ought to know" (1 Cor. 8:1-2).

I always think of one of my seminary professors who referred to an experience that stunned him. The money from his church's Sunday School offering was being pilfered. He was asked to find out who was doing it. The culprit turned out to be the number one verse memorizer in his class. The good professor asked him if he saw any connection between what he was doing and the commandment in Exodus, "You shall not steal."

"Exodus 20:15 to be exact," replied the boy. "No, I don't see any connection."

It took the prof a good half hour to convince the boy that the commandments were for obeying, not just memorizing.

You can't simply memorize God's Word, stow it away for a bad day, and hope the day never comes. The question remains. Once you have memorized the words of Scripture and studied them, what do you do with them?

I believe the next step is meditation on Scripture. Psalm 119 captures the idea this way: "Blessed are they whose ways are blameless, who walk according to the law of the LORD. Blessed are they who keep His statutes and seek Him with all their heart. They do nothing wrong; they walk in His ways. You have laid down precepts that are to be fully obeyed" (vv. 1-4).

Here the psalmist shows that true blessedness—happiness, peace, joy, and love in the Spirit—is gained through observing, walking in, and diligently keeping God's commands. But the real key behind it is revealed in Psalm 119:11: "I have hidden Your word in my heart that I might not sin against You." Part of pleasing God is accomplished through treasuring up the Word in our hearts. It enables us to avoid sin.

It's a picturesque term. To "treasure" carries the idea of hiding something in an assured, cherished place. In those days there were no safes, banks, or vaults where people could put their valuables. Rather, the average fellow would locate a hiding place only he knew about, usually a hole in the floor, a niche in the house, or in a pit in a field. Then he'd hide his wealth there. Robbers lurked about watching for such people so they could steal their valuables.

The psalmist is instructing us to put God's Word in a safe place no one else can see or touch—our hearts. But remember also what you're putting there—something valued and cherished. So in this sense the idea of "treasure" it in your heart is double-edged. Put it in a safe place. But also, cherish the thing you've put there. This leads us to an important tool all Christians need to have in their spiritual kits: meditation on God's Word.

Walking with God in harmony and peace is attained partly by storing His Word in your heart and keeping it as a highly valued item.

In the next few verses, the psalmist amplifies it, saying, "I meditate on Your precepts and consider Your ways. I delight in Your decrees; I will not neglect Your word" (Ps. 119:15-16). Meditation and delight in God's Word is one of those cornerstones we build our lives on. As we allow the Word to color every thought in our minds, we become rainbowed images of Christ. When people observe us they see Him. I believe meditation is the *primary key* to using the Bible in all of life.

The Practice Of Meditation

Recently meditation has gotten a lot of bad press. Gurus do it, then start religions that soon have them traveling about in Rolls Royces. Presumably they meditate in the listless moments between answering their car phones, tending their car bars, and swimming in their car pools (I hear one of them has one).

Monks are supposed to do it. Some orders take vows of silence, poverty, chastity, and every other kind to gain time to meditate and pray.

Even as a non-Christian, I found meditation a weird pastime. I often visited Chapel House, our local university religious center. In the worship area were a number of meditation booths. I used to go in, strip down, sit naked in lotus position, and listen to the night, the sounds of my body, and my mind. I'm not sure what I was trying to do, but it made me feel spiritual. My fraternity brothers were sure I'd gone off the deep end, struck bottom, and broken through.

Since becoming a Christian, I've discovered people have all sorts of ideas about meditation. One man asked if you had to have a special altar to do it. Another wanted a Christian mantra. And others think you must do it in a special booth, like a sauna bath. Some suggest that you take a theological word, like love or peace, and think about it at points during the day. Others take verses, memorize them, and reflect on their meaning when they can. One person I know memorizes hymns and, while singing them, considers the truths imbedded in their rhymes.

Many of these methods are good and worthwhile. Others are downright preposterous and less than biblical. Christian meditation though, is unique; to understand it we must see what Scripture says about the discipline.

King David

Scripture's primary example of the practice of meditation is seen in the life of King David. In Psalm 63, he wrote this: "On my bed I remember You; I think of You through the watches of the night. Because You are my help, I sing in the shadow of Your wings" (Ps. 63:6-7). Can you see David lying on his bed in the wilderness? He's been running from his rebellious son Absalom who threatens to steal the whole kingdom away. His mind races among all the possibilities. He's depressed and fearful, feeling that God has deserted him. At the opening of the Psalm he says, "O God, You are my God, earnestly I seek You; my soul thirsts for You; my body longs for You, in a dry and weary land where there is no water" (v. 1).

Then suddenly he jolts back to reality with the remembrance of his lifelong habit. He begins to meditate on God. He says, "I have seen You in the sanctuary and beheld Your power and Your glory. Because Your love is better than life, my lips will glorify You. I will praise You as long as I live, and in Your name I will lift up my hands. My soul will be satisfied as with the richest of foods; with singing lips my mouth will praise You" (vv. 2-5). He goes back to the days when he stood in the temple, contemplating and praising God's greatness. What exactly was David doing as he lay there in the night, listening to the snores of his loyal kinsmen?

He says that he thought about how God had "been his help." David reviews many of his incredible experiences as God's man: as a shepherd when he struck down the lion and bear; the battle with Goliath; the battles won while a general in King Saul's legions; and the murderous pursuit of King Saul, who threatened to do him in. In each case, David reflects on God's providence: how He protected him, arranged circumstances, used events and persons, and redeemed mistakes and errors—so that all things worked together for his and heaven's good. David also recalls his own feelings in the midst of it. How he nearly gave up in this instance. How he plunged ahead in another, making terrific errors, and yet God still protected him, even from himself.

As David reflects on all these experiences, asking himself questions and reminding himself of what happened, suddenly a song wells up in his soul and he sings for joy. Instantly all the fear evaporates. Absalom and his army begin to look small and insignificant. What appeared to be the end now looks like a new beginning. David weeps into his pillow and thinks, "Oh, God, I should be trusting You. You've always proven Yourself faithful. How can I fear?" He looks up, takes up his shepherd's harp and plays quietly and serenely. Throughout the camp, the frightened women, children, and hardy warriors listen on their own beds. They themselves weep and affirm, "The king's faith has returned." What power meditation has!

In another passage, David praises God with words of power. He says, "they will speak of the glorious splendor of Your majesty, and I will meditate on Your wonderful works" (Ps. 145:5). Here again is a vivid picture. This time David sits in his palace. Maybe he's a little bored. Nothing much is happening. But he begins to reflect again on his

Lord. He decides to offer a great tribute to God in the temple. He will "extol" God, bless Him, and praise Him. What for? First of all for His greatness (Ps. 145:3) — how it's absolutely bottomless, topless, sideless, and endless.

David thinks how he has accomplished so many things in his life — battles won, wives married, wealth gained, promises obtained. But then he compares himself to God. God's greatness is "unsearchable." That is, you can't plumb its depths or surmount its heights. All the libraries in the world couldn't contain enough books to tell of all God has done.

David's heart fills. It's as if his chest cannot contain the joy he's feeling. God is awesome, the King of kings. David remembers the great triumphs of the past, perhaps envisioning the Red Sea parting or Samson slaying a thousand with the jawbone of a donkey. Then he grows silent as he remembers his own sin with Bathsheba, and bows, thankful for God's salvation and forgiveness.

At every turn, David sees the power and majesty of God. Finally, he turns to God's own perfect character. He says, "Of the glorious splendor of Your majesty, . . . I will meditate" (v. 5).

David lay back and enjoyed his reverie. As he meditated, he worshiped. He couldn't help but praise and thank his God in the most eloquent terms he could muster. Imagine him saying to the Lord, "You are great. Your wisdom plunges deep to the severing of soul and spirit. Your perfection no one can fully understand. Your thoughts are so vast and so many, one like me falls back in awe and wonder."

The preceding are some of David's possible thoughts as he penned some individual psalms. I imagine that he reflected on God's qualities and attributes as he experienced them in his life. For example, in Psalm 139 he contemplated the idea that God was watching him day and night. In

Psalm 121 he considered how God never sleeps and guards His children moment by moment. He reflected on God's providence and noted the comfort it brought him.

So much for my musings on the life of David. If you were to meditate on his life and words as portrayed in Scripture you would see and experience different insights. That's the beauty of meditation on God's Word. But one thing is sure. Meditation always leads to worship, for when you meditate you begin to see who God is.

Moses

David wasn't the only meditator in Scripture. Moses penned that greatest of all motivators for meditators: "Hear, O Israel: The LORD our God, the LORD is one. Love the LORD your God with all your heart and with all your soul and with all your strength. These commandments that I give you today are to be upon your hearts. Impress them on your children. Talk about them when you sit at home and when you walk along the road, when you lie down and when you get up. Tie them as symbols on your hands and bind them on your foreheads. Write them on the door-frames of your houses and on your gates" (Deut. 6:4-9).

Moses commanded God's people to fix the Word in their hearts when teaching, talking, walking, and resting—in other words, in all of life. They were to "bind them as a sign on their hands" and put them as "frontals on their foreheads." So all-consuming was their passion for God's Word to be that they were to write it on the doorposts of their houses and on their gates.

Can you imagine such people? Like Tevye in *Fiddler on the Roof*, they're always talking with God, debating, questioning, praying, thinking, and working through old truths and principles. Everywhere they go are reminders of these truths. The fringes of their cloaks are anchored by tassels, each one a symbol of a basic premise of Scripture. As they walk through their doorways, there is a box by the latch containing another reminder that they worship God alone.

Have you ever been in such a home? The presence of Christ permeates everything. Where He is Lord, there is an attitude of love and hospitality that is infectiously attractive.

That's what Moses was getting at. He wanted his people to see the greatness of God and walk about with the glow of God's glory. He didn't desire a simple prayer at dusk, but a conversation all day long with the Lord of creation. Moses was above all a man who meditated on God's truths. He fed on them as the eagle feeds on the fish of the stream. He rejoiced in them as Romeo rejoiced in the eyes of Juliet. Like Job, he desired God's Word more than food itself.

Habakkuk

Another great meditator was Habakkuk. His book is tucked away in the end of the Old Testament, but his words roar with power. As he gazed around at the people of his generation, he saw nothing but wickedness, lust, hatred, murder, and strife. He cried out to God, asking Him to do something. God did. He told Habakkuk He'd send an army of merciless murderers to wipe out the people of Israel.

Habakkuk was aghast. "How can a holy God do such a thing?" he probably asked. "How can You use such evil people?"

That was when Habakkuk began to learn to meditate. If you study the book, You'll see in Habakkuk 1:12 to 2:1 he began asking God a multitude of questions. In his mind he saw nothing but contradictions. On the one side was God's holiness. On the other was this merciless judgment. On the one side was God's justice. On the other was ravage and

plunder. Habakkuk responded by going to the guard post
and waiting for God's answer. But he didn't simply stand
there watching the grass grow. No doubt he thought about
this text and that passage as he tried to discern God's will.
As he weighed them all together he got hopelessly confused and wondered if there was ever any answer.

That's meditation—thinking, questioning, arguing, debating—fighting tooth and nail for your point of view, then
backing down when a new piece of information is revealed.
If anything, meditation is a conversation with God. It's give
and take, weep and shout, pray and praise, hope and dis-
couragement all wrapped together in a bundle of electric
energy.

As Habakkuk meditated, he waited for God to answer.
And God answered with five woes—judgments on all the
wicked. Habakkuk again was stunned. All his meditations
had not led him to this. But that's another thing he was
learning. God's ways aren't our ways. Meditation shows
you that. Through it you begin to think like God. When the
woes were over, Habakkuk slumped with exhaustion. In
the morning, he decided to write everything down. But
after penning the whole history of his prayer, meditation,
and God's answer, something was missing. For Habakkuk
was no longer discouraged, he'd seen something through
his meditations he'd never seen before. Chapter 3 is one of
the fervent psalms of the Bible, ending with the benedic-
tion, "Though the fig tree does not bud and there are no
grapes on the vines, though the olive crop fails and the
fields produce no food, though there are no sheep in the
pen and no cattle in the stalls, yet I will rejoice in the LORD,
I will be joyful in God my Saviour. The Sovereign LORD is
my strength; he makes my feet like the feet of a deer, he
enables me to go on the heights" (vv. 17-19). That's what
meditation does—it gives us deer's feet and enables us to
ascend to the topmost moutains of God's truth. This is why

meditation is such an important tool in unlocking the treasure chests God has for us. Only through meditating on Scripture and God's truth, did David, Moses, and Habakkuk become men of faith and power.

What Is It To Meditate?

There are two words used in Hebrew which we translate, "meditate." One is the root, *hagah*, which means to make a low sound. Isaiah pictures it nicely when he relates it to the moaning of doves (Isa. 59:11) and the growling of a lion over a kill (Isa. 31:4). It also carries the idea of whispering and muttering to oneself (Isa. 8:19). An interesting related term describes the low resounding music on a lyre (Ps. 92:3).

Do you get the picture? To meditate is much like reading a text to yourself. You quietly mouth the words over and over, seeking to gain an understanding of them. But like the quiet melody and background music of a harp, there's a soothing, calming, peaceful aspect to it. You talk to yourself about it and also talk to God in the midst of it.

The second word is *siach*. It means to rehearse, or "go over something in one's mind." It can be inward or outward. That is, one might do such meditation while talking out loud, or simply by listening to the inner voice. The psalmist uses the word in Psalm 119 numerous times, saying he'd meditate on God's precepts and statutes (v. 15, 23, 27, 48, 78). He also speaks of how he anticipates the "night watches, that I may meditate on Thy word" (v. 148, NASB).

You can see the priest standing at his guard post. It doesn't take much concentration to watch for movement in the brush, so he turns to a passage of Scripture. He reviews the words in his mind. He talks to himself, argues, asks a question, prays. He comes to a word that doesn't seem to fit, and says, "Why do You say it this way, Lord?" He turns it over in his mind, inspecting every grammatical construction, striving to understand every syllable and meaning. For him, guard duty was not a nightly struggle to avoid falling asleep. Rather, it was a time when he'd be free, quiet, and able to think on God's Word without interruption.

One way to look at meditation on Scripture is to study several of its results. For instance, in Psalm 77:6, Asaph remembers how he sang in the night, meditated with his heart, and his spirit pondered. To ponder means to "search out," to examine much as a detective inspects for clues at the scene of a crime.

In Psalm 119:15, the writer speaks of how meditation leads one to "consider Your [God's] ways." Again, it's the idea of looking into and considering. In a recent problem at work I was given the job of investigation. I had to go about gathering facts, looking into corners, files, letters, and texts, searching for that one grain of truth that might lead us to a solution. Meditation is like an investigation. It's a fact gathering expedition.

Psalm 119:24 brings a fascinating element to the idea. It says, "Your statutes are my delight; they are my counselors." A counselor offers advice, direction. But here the psalmist refers to God's Word, not a person. Yet, that's exactly what the Word does—it offers counsel. When you meditate on and understand a text, the Spirit can later remind you of it in a problem situation, and suddenly you see what God's will is for that moment. Meditating on the Bible can bring God near in your time of need.

The Strongest Passage Of All

In Proverbs 6:20-23 Solomon exhorts his son to observe the commandments of his father and mother. He says, "My son, keep your father's commands and do not forsake your mother's teaching. Bind them upon your heart forever; fasten them around your neck. When you walk, they will guide you; when you sleep, they will watch over you; when you awake, they will speak to you."

Observing the commandments and binding them on your heart is meditation. But what happens? When you walk about, they guide you. As you're traveling along in life, they offer on the spot counsel for any problem. The Spirit reminds you of the passage and you have direction.

One day I made a tremendous mistake in my business and I was tempted to try to hide it. But immediately, the Spirit brought to mind a verse: "He who conceals his sins does not prosper, but whoever confesses and renounces them finds mercy" (Prov. 28:13).

Since I wanted to prosper, I didn't conceal them. I went to the person involved, confessed them, said I'd stop doing it, and immediately she extended to me full compassion.

More than all of this, "when you sleep, they [the commandments] will watch over you" (v. 22). How does God's Word watch over you? When asleep, you're at your most vulnerable moment. In the days of Solomon, when locks and keys were far from perfected, people were always in great danger from enemies. Solomon is reminding his son that when we obey God's commandments, they become like a hedge or fence about us. God Himself protects us.

In Billy Graham's book, *Angels,* he refers to a missionary who was attacked by natives. Each night the natives waited outside his hut seeking to ambush him. But each night they went away in fear. When they finally became Christians the chief asked the missionary, "Who were the shining ones standing on your porch each night when we came to kill you?" The missionary had been aware of no presence. But he realized that God must have sent "shining ones"—angels—to keep the natives at bay.

Finally, Solomon says, "When you awake, they will talk to you" (v. 22). I find that this is precisely the experience of one who meditates on Scripture. The Scriptures, through the Spirit, talk to us. The Living Word (Jesus) speaks to us through the written Word (the Bible). They provide comfort when we're distressed, counsel when we're afraid, hope when we're discouraged. In every circumstance, the answer comes to one who knows the Word. Meditating, in effect, becomes a doorway to much treasure, for through it the Spirit is given the tools to work in our hearts and minds.

Where Do I Start?

Let me offer a suggestion for beginners. Take a verse you've memorized and as you drive to work or church, turn it over in your mind. Ask the Lord questions about it. Expect Him to answer.

For instance, take a verse we all know, John 3:16, (NASB): "For God so loved the world that He gave His only begotten Son, that whoever believes in Him shall not perish, but have eternal life." Start off by repeating the verse to yourself. Ask questions. What does it mean that "God so loved"? What greater love could God show than to sacrifice His Son? Look for answers in the verses.

Ask another: What does it mean He's the "only begotten Son"? Does it mean He's the only one? You might look up the meaning in a commentary when you get home or think through some other verses related to it. "He is the image of the invisible God, the first-born of all creation" (Col. 1:15, NASB). How might this passage relate?

What does He mean by "the world"? Does He mean just the world of men, or all creation? Does He mean every last man, woman, and child, or only certain ones?

How about this word "believes"? What is it to believe in Christ? What does that involve?

As you go about thinking through and answering these questions, you're engaging in meditation. Often, your meditation will lead you to further study and exploration. You may want to read Bible dictionaries and commentaries to gain more insight.

If anything, meditation is a reflecting on issues and ideas. It's bouncing your ideas off the wall of your mind, then watching them bounce back into your heart with the Holy Spirit's teaching imprint on them. Each time you bounce an idea it will come back a little bigger and you will experience the joy of being *delighted by discipline*.

Start Today

The important point is to start now with what you know. Meditate on a passage. Let the Lord speak to your heart. Make a mental note of the things you want to look up or search out further. Take the time to find answers through your study.

Some time ago I preached a sermon on Matthew 4:1-11, the passage about the temptation of Jesus in the wilderness. For several weeks, because I work in a machinery company, I walked around our complex meditating on the passage. As I turned things over in my mind, it seemed that the Lord flooded me with insight into the text. I pictured much of what happened, got beyond the surface things, and began moving into depths I'd never seen before. As I walked along, I frequently felt like shouting hallelujah to the passing traffic, or grabbing someone by the lapels and saying, "Guess what I learned about Jesus' temptation in the wilderness!"

When I preached the sermon a pastor who heard it com mented that I sounded like I'd spent a lot of time in the passage. He thought my insights showed true depth and had sparked many identifying thoughts in his own mind.

Actually, I hadn't done that much formal study with the books, because I hadn't had time. I'd simply meditated on the text as much as I could those previous weeks. But that meditation time paid off.

Meditation runs the whole gamut of Bible study and experience. It starts with the words of the text and asks, *"What does it say?"* It moves on to the meaning, saying, *"What does it mean?"* Finally, it strikes at the heart of application, saying, *"What does it have to do with me?"* In the process of meditation, you'll hit on all those elements.

But the important thing is that you take the time—while driving, waiting in a line at the store, when drifting off to sleep, or resting on your lunch break—to meditate on a verse or two. In all these settings you can be *delighted by discipline*. Who knows—God may startle you with an insight that would even amaze the Apostle Paul.

Nine

FINDING THE TIME

I bet I know what you're thinking. How can anyone find enough time to engage in all the Bible study, memorization, and meditation necessary to begin applying the Scriptures in all of life? Don't fret, there are some answers.

There is an incredible time crunch upon all of us. Both parents work full-time jobs in more families today than ever before. Activities crowd our schedules. We're more aware today of the need to exercise, diet, save money, invest properly, keep abreast of world events, spend "quality" time with the people in our lives, disciple others, store up treasure in heaven, leave a legacy, and "number our days" that it all seems to tumble down upon us like the water over Niagara Falls.

Meanwhile, the church asks for more of our time and money. Sometimes the Scriptures seem to pour out a steady stream of do this and don't do that to the point that we're all frazzled. We must give more time to our work as well or our careers will fizzle.

In the midst of all this, where does anyone find the time to carve out three hours for Bible study, memorize a whole book of the New Testament, or meditate on a few verses?

On the contrary, perhaps there is a better question: How can one not find the time? Martin Luther once said that he had so much to do on a day that he'd have to pray three hours in the morning or the devil would get the victory. Three hours! Most of us just fire off a mental skyrocket, "Lord, help!" and whiz off to our labors.

One man I know awakens every morning at 5:30 A.M. to study the Bible. Many of us would love to do that. But it's the day after that kills us. Sure, we might do it on Monday. But what happens Tuesday morning when you're still recovering?

But how can you begin using the Bible in all of life unless you give it the time? You can't. It's impossible. You can't apply what you don't know. You can't know what you don't take the time to learn and study. God doesn't infuse our minds with truth. We have to imbibe it—line by line, verse by verse, moment by moment, day by day. How then can anyone find the time?

Prerequisites

This isn't a time management book. If you want to find out how to better organize your day you can find numerous tomes on the subject in any bookstore. But I have discovered that there are numerous ways to find the time, if you're willing to work at it. Let me offer several questions that must be asked in finding the time to learn Scripture on a level that can transform your life.

First, how much do you want to know and apply the Bible to your life? Is it important? Is it a priority? If it's not, you probably wouldn't be reading this book.

But on the other hand, there are many who hope or wish for some secret to make it easy. Very simply, there is no secret. It's not easy. It takes work; it continues to take work; it will always take work. Why? Because we're at the center of the worst battle in history—the battle between God and Satan for each mind, heart, and will born onto Planet Earth. The battle plan of Satan is simple: keep them ✳ from knowing anything about God or His Word. If they do find out, keep them from any commitment. If they do get committed, keep them from following through. If they do follow through, keep them from enduring and influencing others. If they do influence others, keep it to a minimum. Any way. Any how. The ends—hell—justify the means— deceit, disease, destruction, despair.

That battle never ends. Satan has a million ways of diverting us from the Book: TV, movies, food, newspapers, hobbies, work, problems, feelings of inadequacy, fear, you name it. Any way is OK with him.

At the start, the Christian has to decide how important it is to live for the Lord, advance His kingdom, and accomplish His will. If it's not important, then you can do anything you want. But if it is, then you will be faced with a steady barrage of diversions, detours, and roadblocks that Satan will throw in your way to get you sidetracked. Be prepared for it. Expect it. God will give us grace, but we have to receive it too. Regular dependence on God requires as much an act of the will as our initial decision to follow Christ. Thus, if knowing the Word is important, you will find the time because the Spirit of God and your spirit will make sure you have it.

Recently, my wife and I stopped watching television in the evening. Now we read in bed, talk, spend time with the kids. One thing I do is read two to three chapters of the Old Testament, one of the New Testament, and anywhere from four to eight chapters of the passage from my memory review/meditation time that day. It takes anywhere from thirty to sixty minutes. If I was watching television I wouldn't have that time. But just changing my use of those

evening hours from 8:30 to 11:00 transforms everything. I
use the rest of the time to read books and magazines that
keep me informed about my work, world, and faith. I now
look forward to that time. In fact, I count on it. Without it,
I'm sure I'd be spinning flat tires in quicksand.

Second, what are your goals? What do you want to
accomplish in this life? Where are you headed? Dr. Howard
Hendricks frequently advised us in his classes at Dallas
Seminary to write down our goals on paper. "It will transform your life," he said.

It did mine. Before my eyes are a number of long-term
goals that guide me every day in making choices and decisions. A person learns to say "no" on the basis of his or
her goals. Of course, you want to align your goals with
God's plan too, but that requires Bible study. You can't
know what God wants unless you've read what He said He
wants.

Try this: Spend an hour thinking through the achieve-
ments you'd like to look back on when you're ready to
depart this world. What would you want to read in your
obituary? "He knew the TV schedule forward and back-
ward." "She watched every installment of 'The Young and
the Restless.' Didn't miss a one." "He read every James
Bond novel three times." "She spent four hours every day
gossiping on the phone." Or, "He knew the Book and applied it in his life daily."

For today simply review your answer to this important
question. That is what your life will amount to at its end.

Once you've done such an evaluation, begin writing out
the things you would like to accomplish. Establish both
short-term and long-term items. Put the list in your wallet
or purse and consult it regularly. Start working toward
reaching those goals—with prayer and dependence on the
Lord.

Remember this: You can always change a goal. There

may be some you will later realize are nonessential, foolish, or even too grandiose. So establish new ones in their place. No one is setting this paper in concrete. Update it regularly.

Third, what are you willing to cut that will enable you to reach your goals? Already you've noticed your day is full. So to reach your goals concerning the Bible, you'll probably have to make some changes. The easiest step is to get rid of the waste. The fat. Like the author to the Hebrews says, "Throw off everything that hinders, and the sin which so easily entangles" (Heb. 12:1-2). Why? So you can run the race.

Ever watch the running heats in a track meet? What are those competitors wearing—balloon shirts, sombreros, and high heels? No way, they're stripped down—in fact to the bare minimum. They don't want anything hindering them from running all out.

Look at your day like a hundred meter dasher looks at his race. Strip it down. Refine it. Get it into top order. Use some discipline. Pare away. What? TV is a biggie. And so are videos. Do you spend too much time in the newspaper? What about gabbing on the phone? And don't forget listening to the radio.

I'm not saying recreation is wrong, or useless, or even godless. But much of the time we spend in frivolity as citizens of the Hollywood culture could be used for God's kingdom.

After you've cut out the waste, start in on making choices between what is good, what is better, and what is best. Dr. Hendricks told us that as we increased our work for the Lord, we would be assaulted with people wanting us to do all sorts of things—good, admirable, and worthy things.

But you can't do it all. You have to make choices. Which ones are the best choices? Which library books—out of millions—should be read? Which Bible verses—out of thousands—should be memorized first? Which ministry opportunities—out of several—should be taken on?

As you grow in the Christian life you quickly find that if Satan can't wipe you out with sin, he'll destroy you with too much good! He'll use the church to pile on activities till you're crushed. He'll lead others to offer you ripe opportunities to divert you from real kingdom goals.

Once you've cut out the waste and the simply good and better things to leave only the best, there's one more step: Learn to continually redeem the time.

I once heard a story about a man who got a call from his bank saying someone had deposited $1,000 in his name. In order to get it, all he had to do was come down, claim it, and spend it all that same day. The man, overjoyed, went down to pick up the money and had a fine time spending it.

But the next morning he got another call. Another $1,000. Same conditions. He sped down and repeated his efforts.

Third morning, same scenario. Now the man was getting a little concerned. He asked, "How long will this go on?"

The banker didn't know. "This could be the last one today. It might not. I have no guarantees."

The man responded, "If this is going to keep happening, I'm going to have to do some planning. I can't just spend $1,000 every day of my life on a lark."

The banker agreed, but said that was his business.

The man sat down and tried to think of what to do. He didn't just want to dribble it all away, but he had to spend the full amount that day or it would be gone—lost forever—at the end.

What's the point? If you sleep about seven and half hours a night, you have just about 1,000 minutes to spend each day. You can't store it up or save it. You have to use it minute by minute. But how? Investing it in God's kingdom is the answer. Redeeming the time is the application.

To redeem the time means to buy it back out from under another owner. Paul speaks to this issue: "Be very careful, then, how you live—not as unwise but as wise, making the most of every opportunity, because the days are evil" (Eph. 5:15-16).

"Making the most of every opportunity"—that's redeeming the time. How do you do that? Through wisdom, insight, and understanding. How do you gain those three capacities? Through the Word of God.

It becomes a circle. You can only redeem the time through being wise, insightful, and full of understanding. You can only be wise, insightful, and understanding through studying the Word of God. When you study the Bible you will learn to redeem the time in all things.

Some Practical Hints

What are some practical hints for redeeming the time? Let me offer five suggestions I've found to be helpful.

1. Learn to be realistic. Don't try to do too much. Make "faith-sized" goals. These are goals that you really believe God can accomplish in you. They're not so big that you think they're impossible to attain. But they also require faith—on your own you couldn't accomplish them.

Bounce your goals off a few friends. Ask them if they think they're realistic considering your gifts, faith, and previous record.

2. Learn to double up. Figure out ways to do mind-involving activities while you're doing something requiring less concentration. When I'm driving on the highway I do a number of things. One is to spend time praying and meditating on passages of Scripture. Each morning, during that forty-five minute drive to work, and in the afternoon on the way home, I go over anywhere from four to nine chapters of the Bible which I've memorized. I repeat them back in my head and meditate on them as I'm driving. I'm almost afraid to move closer to work for fear of losing that block of time I can always count on for meditation!

You can also listen to tapes in the car—tapes of books, sermons, teaching, music, etc. It can become a source of tremendous learning and edification.

Standing in lines—how often are we doing that? You can spend that time meditating, praying, reading, and thinking.

What about cutting the lawn, sunbathing, holding on the phone, waiting for the computer, even watching TV! They can all be times when you stop to pray (during a commercial, for instance) or engage in a redemptive activity.

Learn to double up everywhere you can. You will find that these are prime times for spiritual work in the kingdom.

3. Take charge of your day at the start. Charles Schwab, president of Bethlehem Steel, was approached by a consultant named Ivy Lee about a way to get more work done. Lee offered him a plan that involved (1) writing down the six most important tasks to do the next day, (2) numbering them in order of importance, and (3) then doing them in that order. As an addendum, the fourth step was to realize that any that weren't done could be left till the next day. Lee asked Schwab to use the system himself. Once he thought it was worthwhile, he could pay Lee whatever he felt it was worth.

A few weeks later, Schwab sent Lee a check for $25,000.

The system has become a standard in time management seminars. The only way to win over these days that are so fraught with evil is to take charge of them yourself each morning. Otherwise, emergencies, other people, and your own weaknesses and natural laziness will take over. You'll fritter your time away to nothing.

4. Use your schedule for spiritual activity. Your drive to and from work can be a time of worship, meditation, education, or other activity. Don't use your lunchtime for more work at your desk; use it for God's kingdom. By clearing out your head with a noontime walk, fresh air, meditation, and time in prayer, you may actually accomplish more that afternoon because you've filled yourself with God's truth and power. If you have two fifteen-minute breaks a day, again use them for good.

I've found that when I add up my two forty-five-minute commutes, one-hour lunch, and two fifteen-minute breaks, I have up to three hours of *my* time which I control that can be invested in work for God's kingdom. Learn to use your present schedule for God's glory. Similarly, Paul exhorts us: "So whether you eat or drink or whatever you do, do it all for the glory of God" (1 Cor. 10:31). Everything in life can count for His glory.

5. Know yourself. When are you most alert? This may be the best time to handle spiritual matters. Is it the morning? The evening? Lunchtime? Know yourself. Know when you're up and when you're down. Study yourself to see what the best way of using time is. Fit your spiritual life into your personality quirks and traits so that you are giving it your best part of the day. It's through knowing yourself that you eventually see how to best use all your spiritual gifts.

Get On With It

None of us is equal in any way—in abilities, intelligence, financial power, strength—except one. Time. We all have twenty-four hours in which to live today. There's no such thing as not enough time. There are only people who don't manage the time they have properly.

So get on with it. And realize that Jesus is at your right hand, doing all He can to bring you to maximum success.

Ten

PUTTING
THE
SCRIPTURES
INTO
LIFE

How then do you get God's truth into every nook and cranny of your life?

It will be a battle. It will not be easy. It will mean lots of pain, hurt, and change. Others will reject, persecute, and hate you. The battle will never end. It will go on right up to the end. But it is a battle that can be won, a battle where you can daily be on the winning side. This chapter is about how to do it.

What I'm Not Talking About

It is not riding the crest of a wave of victory. Some believers think the Christian life should be one incredible high, one astonishing victory after another. I don't see that Jesus had that kind of life, let alone any of us. There are setbacks and advances every day when you walk with Jesus. As Charles Swindoll writes, it's three steps forward, two steps back. I'm not suggesting that every day will be better than the day before if you apply these principles. Life just isn't that way.

It is not gradually growing toward a certain point either. You might think that there are setbacks now, but eventually you will reach a point where everything goes right.

Sorry. That's not the way it is either. None of us will ever, in this life, reach a point where we've arrived, where we simply move from high to high. That may be in heaven, but not here.

It is not even hoping for perfection in this life. Are you hoping to reach that marvelous plane where everything goes great? That's the longing for the Second Coming. But it has nothing to do with this life. Forget it. We're in a war.

What I Am Talking About

It is a marathon in which we reach the end by grace alone. One of my profs used to say, "The Christian life isn't a hundred-yard dash; it's a marathon." Oh, we'll get there. We'll be tired, just dragging in, wondering if we'll make it. But we will reach the end. God's going to get us there. That's why Jude said, "To Him who is able to keep you from falling and to present you before His glorious presence without fault and with great joy" (Jude 24).

Anyone who wants to apply the Bible in all of life will do so only at the expense of total commitment and energy and only because the Spirit of God has effected it by His grace.

So then, how do you begin applying the Bible in all of life? Let me offer you several potent and time-tested guidelines.

The First And Always Question

The first question a Christian should ask about any subject, or while facing any problem is this: What does the Bible say about it? It may take awhile to define the problem precisely. It might require some study to focus the issue. It may even be an issue that the Bible does not speak to directly. But the Bible will have answers. It's the first place to go, and the only source we can rely on absolutely.

I'm amazed at the places I've seen myself turn when I'm frustrated over some issue that has popped into my life. Anger, complaining, wishes in the night, and stout denials that any problem exists have all been common places to start. After that, if it doesn't go away, I've turned to psychologists, doctors, parents, friends, pastors, and teachers. I've tromped over to the local Christian bookstore and purchased every book on the subject. But eventually I find that I have to go to the Bible. And inevitably it has some answer, however palatable or distasteful.

Now why don't I—and most of us who claim to be Christians—start there? Our sinful nature is the problem. It is the tendency to look for the easy way out—the hunger for a "quickie fix." But it never works. And the Word always does—if we apply it properly.

The secret of using the Bible in all of life is asking the question, "What does the Bible say about it?" Abortion, human rights, principles about voting, marriage to a non-Christian, AIDS, depression, anger, fear, loneliness—you name it, you can find principles about it in the Scriptures. They may not be direct answers to an issue. Actually, the Bible rarely addresses specific issues. Rather, it gives you the tools and rules with which to deal with them. It's the classic trouble-shooting manual.

What is the goal? "To purify for Himself a people that are His very own, eager to do what is good" (Titus 2:14). It's purity. Being His very own. Being eager to do what's good. That's where it's all leading. That will be the essence of His kingdom when it comes.

This is why our first reaction should always be "What does the Bible say about it?"

The only true security we have in this world is the Bible. What can you truly count on in this world? The government? Our leaders? Science? The "wisdom of the ages"? Traditions? Friends? Family? The bestseller list? Hollywood? The Church? Other Christians? Ultimately, every one of those sources will break down, lose courage, offer faulty advice, fail, betray, or even turn around and do you in.

But the Bible is the single sure rock in all of this. It can be relied upon absolutely. Its words will never fade. Its promises never fail. Its truth is as secure today as it was the moment the prophet's ink dried on the sheepskin. Martin Luther said, "The Bible is alive, it speaks to me; it has feet, it runs after me; it has hands, it lays hold on me." Christian Karl Bunsen said, "The Bible is the only cement of nations, and the only cement that can bind religious hearts together." Timothy Dwight spoke of it this way: "The Bible is a window in this prison-world, through which we may look into eternity." Billy Graham called it, "The constitution of Christianity."[1]

I gave a young man in my church a pocket Bible when he went away to Wabash College. Three weeks later I saw him again and in our conversation he whipped out that little Bible to quote something. I hardly listened to the quote; I was staring at the Bible. The covers were torn, the pages dogeared. There was scrawling all over it. It looked like it was forty years old. I asked him what on earth he'd been doing with it. He said, "Well, I carry it around with me in my back pocket everywhere I go because I'm always looking up stuff. I guess it got that way from being with me all the time."

That's the mentality. It's "with me all the time." The kind of condition we need to get our Bibles in is: USED!

How do you get this perspective? It's a matter of choice,

---

[1]The Quiet Heart, *Decision*, May, 1977.

practice, and habit. Ask the Holy Spirit to remind you to think "Bible" in response to every question, issue, and need—whether it's in the office or home, on the playing field, or out in the parking lot. It's an attitude, an outlook that must be nurtured and cultivated.

In fact, it's this very quality that separates Christians from the rest of the world. Remember what Paul said? "We are fools for Christ's sake" (1 Cor. 4:10, NASB). What was it that distinguished such a fool? A reliance and dependence on God and His wisdom as revealed in the Word.

The world will scorn and deride anyone who seriously consults the Bible about things. But it is one thing that guarantees God's favor and blessing.

Apply The Word

The goal of all Bible study is application. My wise professor, Dr. Hendricks—whom you must be thinking by now influenced me more than anyone else on earth—used to say, "Observation and interpretation without application is abortion!" How true. The Bible is not a databank or an encyclopedia you use just to gain knowledge; it's a living Word from God meant to change our lives. It must be studied, understood, and *applied.*

Years ago I came up with an acrostic that helped me find the application in any text of Scripture. I called it my *SAFEPACK.* It works like this. Is there a . . .

S — Sin to avoid?
A — Action to do?
F — Faith to exercise?
E — Example to follow?
P — Promise to claim?
A — Attitude to change?
C — Challenge to meet?
K — Key to victory in my life today?

It doesn't solve all the problems of application, but it's a start. As I mentioned at the end of chapter 8, there are three questions to ask. In studying the Bible, you're asking the question, "What does it say?" In interpretation, you want to know, "What does it mean?" But application queries, "What does it have to do with me?" How can you apply this truth to your life?

Recently, I noticed myself becoming a bit irritable around my wife and children. I began reading Ephesians and noticed this verse: "Be kind and compassionate to one another, forgiving each other, just as in Christ God forgave you" (4:32). The word there for "compassionate" means "tenderhearted." Have a tender heart toward those around you. Someone else put it this way: "Be kind; everyone you meet is fighting a hard battle." Consider the battle others are facing and exercise a little compassion. That's what I ended up telling myself. I asked the Lord to make that truth a reality in my life.

I can't say I'm a new man in that regard, but I am seeing change. There's a little more tenderheartedness—some laughter, some tears, some sharing with the little ones.

When you study the Bible, always ask yourself one question: "What can I apply from this passage in my life today?"

I was typing away recently when our newborn baby Alisha Ann began crying for her midday snack. I was on a writing roll, so I heated up a bottle and asked my five-year-old to help feed her. I watched out of the corner of my eye as Nicole held the bottle in Alisha's lips.

As I sat there, I was thinking, "Mark, is this kindness? Is this tenderheartedness? Look at how Nicole has that bottle jammed in there. It looks like she's trying to stop the gush from the Dutch dike. Alisha appears uncomfortable and . . . "

That was enough. I knew I was being selfish, pure and

simple. I got up and took the baby into the family room and fed her.

Afterward, I got on another writing roll and Nicole came in to report something to me. I half listened and said yes, go ahead. She looked at me funny and I realized I hadn't heard a word she'd said. Again, that verse socked me in the jaw: "Be kind, compassionate."

I stopped Nicole and asked her to explain again. It was a good thing too. She had decided to rearrange the family room and wondered if it would be all right with me!

After that, I got back onto the computer and once again, Nicole sashayed in. This time it was, "Daddy, I'm hungry."

"You just ate," I said, between clicks of the keyboard.

"But I didn't have any lunch."

I tried to think up an excuse to tell her to wait till dinner. But I said, "You didn't?" She shook her head. I looked at my watch. It was 4 P.M. I gulped and thanked the Lord for the last part of that verse: "just as in Christ God forgave you."

Always remember to make a conscious effort to apply the Scriptures. Ask yourself, how does what you've studied relate to your life right now.

Biblical Problem-Solving

A third way to begin getting the Bible into your life is to practice biblical problem-solving. That is, define a problem you're having and find out what the Bible says about it. This is similar to my first point, but it's a bit more specific. In this realm, you have isolated a specific problem you're facing. Your goal is to find out what the Scriptures say about it, and then try to apply them to your situation.

My wife and I have been doing this each evening as we read the Bible and have a family worship time after dinner. We've been going through Proverbs. In the process of

reading five to ten Proverbs a night, we can usually find
one or two verses that touch on something we're facing
each day.

Biblical problem-solving works from problem to Scripture. Simply start with the problem and look for an answer
in the Scriptures. It is just as proper to move from the
Bible to a problem (which is really the process of application, as in point two above).

Either way, the goal is to solve your problems biblically.
Biblical problem-solving does not mean you avoid other
sources besides the Bible. Going to a bookstore and picking up a book on your problem is wise. You can find material there on nearly any subject. It will help you isolate
verses more quickly, and also offer you another's perspective and insight on the problem.

I once talked with a famous preacher about his personal
methodology in discipleship. He mentioned that one of the
primary things he teaches his disciples is biblical problem-
solving. He and his disciple would define a problem. Then
he would give him a list of five to ten books to read on the
subject, with an emphasis on studying the Scriptures cited.
Afterward, they would spend time discussing the problem,
how the disciple tried to solve it, what steps he'd taken,
and what answers he'd received.

That's a simple outline. Anyone can follow it. But it's
nothing less than the same process Jesus took His own
disciples through. You can see it in how He would teach
the Twelve, then send them out to apply what He'd taught.
They'd report back later to examine how things had gone.

Cliff Barrows, of the Billy Graham Evangelistic Association, was once flying in a helicopter above the rice paddies
in Korea. He marveled at how straight the lines of rice
were. He wondered how the people did it. His guide told
him that when the people plant the seed they put down a
string stretched out straight just beneath the water. By that

marker, they can keep the lines of rice straight.

Biblical problem-solving is like that. You stretch the line of the Word out underneath you. Then you follow it. In time, you see the ripe, straight fruit of godliness growing in your life.

Make It The Main Topic

A fourth step in the process is an application from Deuteronomy 6:4-9. There, as we noted earlier, Moses instructed the people to put the principles and laws of God on their hearts and then teach them at all times. What was Moses saying? See the truth behind everything that happens, and use it as an opportunity to discuss God's Word.

One of my friends in seminary was like that. We'd be walking down the sidewalk, he'd notice some child shooting a basketball, and he'd comment, "That's the truth of Romans 3:23: we all miss the mark." Or he'd see some father bending over listening to his four-year-old, and he'd say, "That's like it says in Psalm 40:1, how God inclines His ear to listen to us." He had a Scripture for everything.

That's the process of teaching your children, and yourself. Look at life and see the analogy to Scripture.

I was working with someone in a counseling situation, trying to persuade him of a problem that I felt existed, but which he refused to accept. Others had told him repeatedly that he needed to change in this area. But suddenly I said, "What you're doing here is the picture of Proverbs 29:1, 'A man who hardens his neck after much reproof will suddenly be broken beyond remedy' " (NASB). He had to sit up a moment and listen to that one!

Again, when my wife was in labor recently, I couldn't help reflecting on Genesis 3:16 where God told Eve that because of her sin He would "greatly increase your pains in childbearing." (With compassion in mind, I didn't mention it to my wife at the time, but I did think about it.)

Still another insight struck as I watched my days fritter away during a vacation time: "The days are evil" (Eph. 5:16). Evil overtakes everything, and unless you redeem it—buy it out from evil through godly planning and organization—you're on the way to frittering away a whole life.

Anyone who memorizes Scripture long can't help but see connections to the things that happen every day. The Holy Spirit will bring them to mind. Talk about your discoveries. Soon you will find that others in your family are seeing the same truths worked out in experience. When you see truth come alive in the context of your own life you will never forget it.

The Place Of Prayer

Finally, one more thought for applying the Scriptures in all of life: Learn to pray through the Word. Turn the Scriptures into a roadmap for prayer. Use them as your guide. Pray them back to the Father asking Him to make the truth of what you're reading a reality in your life.

As a person who was once in the professional ministry, but now works in a secular job, I find a terrific tension. On the one hand, I'm pulled in the direction of wanting to be back in the pulpit. On the other hand, I realize I'm in the frontlines of the battle in ways that a pastor can never be.

It's a struggle. It became such a battle recently that I had to reach back to some of those Scriptures about work as a help: Colossians 3:22-25; Ephesians 6:5-8; 1 Timothy 6:1-2; and Ecclesiastes 9:10. I found myself impotent to obey those commands, try as I would. But then I turned it all back into prayer. I asked the Lord to grant me the grace to make those words a reality in my life and work.

It's amazing. The going's still tough. It seems that each day I walk into a hailstorm of problems, paperwork, and

people bent on snowing me under. But I find that by looking at what the Scripture says and asking the Lord to apply
it in my work, change comes. Already there's a new buoy-
ancy instead of getting up and slogging into work. There's
a sense of challenge. There's a realization that God put me
here for a reason and I can trust that applying His Word to
the problems will help me overcome. I come back to His
sovereignty each day, thinking that everything is ordered
by Him for a purpose. Therefore I can trust that as I face
the difficulties with the sword of the Spirit, I'll advance.
Three steps forward, two back.

I can't say enough about what it has meant to learn to
use the Bible in all of life. I only wish I could do it more.
I'm confident I will learn as time goes on. Anyone who
applies the Word diligently will see God's blessing. "How
can a young man keep his way pure? By keeping it according to Thy word. With all my heart I have sought Thee; do
not let me wander from Thy commandments" (Ps. 119:9-
10, NASB).

Eleven

TOOLS
FOR
THE
ROAD
AHEAD

Are there any other tools that one can use in making the Bible a part of all of life? In this chapter let me offer you several tools you can use in your daily life that can make it not only exciting, but a moment by moment adventure.

One of the first things you'll want to do is establish yourself in a regular reading program of the Bible. There are a number of methods you can use to read through the Bible in one year. Walk Thru the Bible Ministries has excellent materials and devotional guides that enable you to read through the whole Bible, (or either the New Testament or Old Testament) in a year.

Many Christians set out to do this but never succeed. The key is a support group. If you can get together a group of friends at your church or Bible study to lend support and encouragement, you'll find yourself making the mark.

I use a threefold system in my reading program. One of my goals is to read through the Old Testament once a year, every year. That means reading two to three chapters every day.

The second element is to read through the whole New

Testament once a year also. That requires about one chapter a day.

Finally, I try to read over the same material I've meditated on during my morning drive to work. That's another five to ten chapters of various books of the New Testament. I do this so that as I go over the passages I've memorized I can make sure that I haven't been adding or dropping any verses or phrases. It reinforces the material I've already memorized.

All this reading can be done in twenty to forty minutes a night. I do it in the evening, between 9:00 and 11:00. The fascinating element of it all is that I find the passages always yield up something new and fresh. Sure, I can find myself reading along and not really imbibing anything. To avoid that I've learned to have a quiet time with no distractions. Also, I have to repeatedly force myself to concentrate. It's a battle, and not one easily won. But the more you discipline yourself the greater delight you'll find in the Bible.

I'm convinced the key to knowing the Bible is repetition. It's repeating the readings and hearing the same truths quoted over and over that causes God's truth to sink in. That's why Peter said, "So I will always remind you of these things, even though you know them and are firmly established in the truth you now have" (2 Peter 1:12). Each time we read the Word, it is driven a little more deeply into our souls. Eventually, nothing can dislodge God's truth.

There are other types of reading programs though. One that I learned from John MacArthur, the well-known pastor and teacher, is a process in which you read the same chapters (four to six) every day for a whole month. That is, you take a whole book, like Philippians, or part of a book, like the first seven chapters of John, and read them through every day for the full month. After a few days it seems to get a bit repetitious, but if you hang tough, you find that those truths knit themselves deep into the fabric of your mind. It's that kind of repetition that fixes a book permanently in your psyche.

The beauty of this is that you can read through the whole New Testament approximately thirty times! That's just enough to turn you into a walking Bible. And considering that the famed preacher G. Campbell Morgan used to read a book of the Bible forty times before he preached on it, it's clearly a wise practice.

Tapes And Videos

There are bookworms, and there are tapeworms. Unfortunately, I'm both. But seriously, nothing has proved to be a more powerful resource for my own spiritual life than listening consistently to tapes by Bible teachers. Listening to tapes gives you a chance to hear great men or women of God deliver their best messages to you in an easy-to-understand format. One suggestion: While studying a particular book of Scripture, simultaneously listen to a tape series on that same book by a noted preacher.

Many churches have their own tape ministries. One lending library that I think is excellent is called "Bible Believer's Cassettes." You can write them at 130 North Spring Street, Springdale, Arkansas 72764. They feature a broad selection of tapes from many of today's best preachers.

The beauty of listening to tapes is that you can do it anywhere—in your car, at the beach, at home, etc. A Walkman cassette player taken on a trip around the neighborhood can give you some spiritual food for thought while you exercise.

In the same way, I've also started using videos. It takes more concentration and effort, but through them you can be transported right into a worship setting.

Tools Of The Trade

Another application which offers a high payoff on a small amount of work is the learning of the Greek and Hebrew alphabets. Without knowing anything else about Greek or Hebrew, whole vistas open up to you that were once closed. There are a number of tools available today which can be used effectively by anyone who knows the alphabets well enough to look up words in Greek and Hebrew lexicons and concordances.

Following are some helpful books you might use in your study.

The NIV Interlinear Greek-English New Testament (Alfred Marshall, Zondervan, 1976). This book prints the actual Greek New Testament and places a literal English translation underneath each word. On the side panel is the NIV text. With this tool you can identify the precise Greek word from which we get our English translation. Once you locate it, you can look up the Greek word in the next tool (dictionary) to get the full definition and all the nuances. However, the Greek words in the Interlinear will not be the same as the "root" word which you would have to find in the dictionary. Verbs and nouns will have different prefixes, suffixes, and spellings depending on the exact use in the context. Nonetheless, you can frequently figure out the "root" by the word as it appears in the Interlinear. If not, you can always use two other tools that will help you in that area.

A Greek-English Lexicon of the New Testament (Waltor Bauer, trans.; William Arndt and F. Wilbur Gingrich, University of Chicago Press, 1957). This is a lexicon, a dictionary that lists each use of each Greek word in the New Testament alphabetically. Of course, it lists the word by its "root" spelling, so just looking at the word as it appears in the Interlinear above will not always help, though, as I said, you can often figure it out. But the next tool will help in that area.

An Index to the Bauer-Arndt-Gingrich Greek Lexicon (John R. Alsop, Zondervan, 1958). This index lists each verse in the New Testament and under the verse lists the words in the sentence as they appear in the *B-A-G Lexicon*. It will even tell you the page number and where the word is found in the definition outline as well as which quadrant the word is found in. It's a highly useful tool and can be easily employed by anyone who learns the Greek alphabet. With it you can look up virtually any word in the New Testament and find where it's listed in the lexicon.

However, if the word use is not listed in the *B-A-G Lexicon*, as some are not, then one more tool will help you in that area.

The Analytical Greek Lexicon (Zondervan, 1970). This lexicon lists every spelling found in the Greek New Testament, and with it gives you the declensions of nouns and adjectives, and the conjugations of verbs. After this, it gives you the root spelling. So even if the Index above doesn't list the word, you can always find it listed here. Also, if you take the time to learn a little grammar, you can quickly find other facts about the word with this tool. All of it makes for most fascinating Bible study.

The Englishman's Greek Concordance of the New Testament (Zondervan, 1970). This is a standard concordance that lists each usage of a word by its root. With it you can compare all the different ways one Greek word is rendered into English.

Young's Analytical Concordance to the Bible (Robert Young, Eerdmans, 1964). This concordance is most useful in identifying the original words, because it lists the English words with both the Hebrew and Greek that the King James translates.

These six tools make it possible for even a novice to be

handling the original Greek of the Bible. In effect, you will be enabled to mine out the silver and gold of the great texts just as Luther and Calvin did.

The same kinds of tools are also available for studying Hebrew.

Hebrew and English Lexicon of the Old Testament (Brown, Driver, and Briggs, Oxford University Press, 1907). This is the standard Hebrew lexicon.

Index to Brown, Driver, and Briggs Hebrew Lexicon (Bruce Einspahr, Moody Press, 1976). This is the same kind of index as the one above and lists most of the important words in a verse, as well as their roots, what page and quadrant it's found on in the lexicon, and what part of the definition outline. This is an incredibly useful tool to anyone, even scholars, who find the many forms and spellings of Hebrew words difficult.

Analytical Hebrew and Chaldee Lexicon of the Old Testament (Benjamin Davidson, MacDonald Publishing company). Again, this is similar to *The Analytical Greek Lexicon* above in that it lists every spelling found in the Hebrew, gives its declension or conjugation, and supplies the spelling of its root in the Brown, Driver, and Brigg's lexicon.

The Englishman's Hebrew and Chaldee Concordance (Zondervan, 1970). A concordance on each Hebrew root, listing it by stem (which is the particular Hebrew verb form).

Again, simply by knowing the order of the Hebrew alphabet, all these tools can become highly useful and effective in the life of one who is willing to study and work at it.

The beauty of both these Hebrew and Greek tools is that new avenues to the Bible are opened that would be closed to one who uses only the English. You can do important word studies and find interesting relations among words that you could never get from the English text.

For instance, in Hebrew the word for God's loyal love (*chesed*) is the same root used for the Hebrew word for "stork." The European stork, which would have been seen in Israel, is the kind that builds its nest on housetops and is extremely loyal and gentle with its young. This can be turned into a powerful illustration, not only of the majesty of the Hebrew language, but the fact that the Holy Spirit made such a connection in Scripture. The stork becomes a potent example of God's loyal love.

Similarly, in the Greek, you will discover that there are two words for "good" common in the New Testament: *agathos* and *kalos*. In the English, there is only one word for "good." But in the Greek, there is a distinction. *Agathos* means good in character, something that is beneficial to others. *Kalos* means something intrinsically good, something beautiful, even perfect, something that is ethically good and noble. In fact, another useful tool, W.E. Vine's *Expository Dictionary of New Testament Words* (Revell, 1940) points out the differences in nuance among many Greek words quickly, and lists them by the King James translation. You can trace through the usage of such words and find many fascinating nuances of meaning that will broaden you spiritually and mentally.

A Study Retreat

Finally, the *study retreat* can be an effective discipline. Retreats have been a mainstay for many churches. They're a beautiful time to meet new Christians, rekindle old friendships, and simply get away.

But there is another kind of retreat. The purpose of a study retreat is to get alone with the Lord for a few days. Many college campuses (Christian and secular) have special centers where people can come to meditate, write, think, walk, and simply commune with the quiet.

You can find such retreat centers with everything from loose to highly-fixed schedules. One center might have sessions everyday; others might simply let you do your own thing. Choose what best fits your needs.

When I was considering college, my first choice was Colgate University largely because of a retreat center they have on campus called "Chapel House." It featured a large religious library, a small quiet chapel with meditation booths, and rooms downstairs for people to stay for a weekend, a week, or longer. The rates were low and it was an excellent getaway.

Investigate your local area for some college, church, or community that has such a center. A study retreat can become a time of great renewal in your own life and in the life of your family.

So Many Tools

God has filled our world with all sorts of good things that can help us make the Bible a part of all of life. Look around you. Find the tools that are effective for you and use them. Books, tapes, videos, and study retreats are only a few. Discover what works for you. The important thing is that you use it to advance yourself in the kingdom and become more attuned to God's Word and His ways. So go at it. And have some fun while you're doing it.

Twelve

EQUIPPED
FOR
LIFE

Where are we headed in seeking to use and apply the Bible in all of life? Paul summed it up in one of his letters: "All Scripture is God-breathed and is useful for teaching, rebuking, correcting, and training in righteousness, so that the man of God may be thoroughly equipped for every good work" (2 Tim. 3:16-17).

I find that I have to remind myself of this truth constantly. But this passage, while one of the most important texts on the inspiration and infallibility of Scripture, subtly reveals the end of all our labors: to be "thoroughly equipped for every good work."

What does this verse teach about the effort we put into learning and inculcating the Bible into our lives?

The first thing to notice is that Paul says "all Scripture is God-breathed." Although Paul was referring to the Scriptures as they were available at that time in history—the Old Testament—he was making a generic statement. He meant that any and all places in which God has communicated to us by revealed and Spirit-expired truth are useful.

That means even those difficult books—Leviticus and

Amos, Hebrews and 3 John—are useful. We can gain insight and help from them no matter how difficult they
might seem to us at first.

I remember a friend who was studying and memorizing
in Isaiah over a period of nearly two years. He remarked to
me that in most of the counseling he'd been doing during
that time, he was turning to Isaiah to give the counselee
spiritual guidance. I was a bit astonished. I thought he
would be using mostly Paul's epistles. But here was someone turning to Isaiah quite regularly.

I had another friend who was converted through doing
Hebrew exegesis of the Book of Genesis. He had a scientific background. One of the greatest stumbling blocks to
faith in Christ for him was the theory of evolution and
recent scientific discovery. He decided he had to find out if
the Bible was true, so he taught himself Hebrew, then began doing Hebrew exegesis in chapters 1 and 2 of Genesis!
In the process he became a believer and later went to
seminary.

Remember, *all* Scripture is useful.

God-Breathed

The next thing Paul says is that it's "God-breathed." Other
texts translate it "inspired." But the idea of the Greek
word is that God breathed out the words of Scripture.
What happens when we talk? We breathe out over our
vocal chords and words are formed. The Scriptures are the
"breathings out" of God.

But there's something more here. What happened when
God breathed out into something else? When God breathed
into Adam, the Scripture says he became a living being. In
the same way, the words of the Bible actually possess the
life of God. They're "living and active" as Hebrews 4:12
says. That means that when you read the Bible, you're

hearing, receiving, touching, imbibing, and experiencing the actual power and life of God Himself. Those words, unlike others on the printed page anywhere else, are specially inspired by God.

Useful

Scripture is also described as being "useful." The word means beneficial, profitable. The words of the Bible have an immediate as well as a long-term effect. They profit the person who is exposed to them.

Paul's meaning is more than just words that can help you out. The same word was used in Matthew 16:26 where Jesus is recorded as saying "What good will it be for a man if he gains the whole world, yet forfeits his soul?" If you measure the profit of the whole world against a soul the latter far outweighs the former. That's rather high profit.

But in other texts (see 1 Cor. 13:3, 14:6; 1 Tim. 4:8; Titus 3:8) the idea is of something far greater, something that changes a person inside, something that so utterly transforms that one is not the same again. And isn't that precisely what Scripture does?

When D.L. Moody held evangelistic services in St. Louis, he preached on the Philippian jailer in Acts 16. The next day, the local paper *The Globe Democrat* published a story entitled, "How the Jailer at Philippi Was Caught." That issue of the paper fell into the hands of one of the worst criminals of the day, Valentine Burke, who was incarcerated in the city prison. He had already spent more than half his life behind bars, and to see this kind of headline was a thrill for him. He read the story enthusiastically, jubilant at the thought of a jailer getting caught in a crime. He had also heard of a town in Illinois called Philippi, so he thought this must be the locale of the seizure.

But the article didn't tell him much of the supposed

capture; rather, he kept running over the words, "Believe in the Lord Jesus Christ and you will be saved" (Acts 16:31, RSV). He finally threw the paper down in disgust, remarking that it was nothing but a bunch of "religious stuff."

That might have been the end of it. But for Valentine Burke it wasn't. He couldn't get those words out of his mind: "Believe in the Lord Jesus Christ and you will be saved." As he sat in his lonely cell, his whole immoral past seemed to buzz through his mind. He even imagined the day of judgment and what he would be called to account for. Finally, he bowed and accepted Jesus, just as that original jailer had. He went on to become a potent witness for the Lord, even though he remained behind bars.

God's Word transforms. You can't be indifferent to it. It may enrage you. It may encourage you. It may wait and strike at a moment when you're not thinking about it. But it will never "return to Me [God] empty," as Isaiah says (Isa. 55:11).

The Scope Of This Power

Now notice the scope of the Bible's power. It provides "teaching." That's the mental component. Through that teaching you gain knowledge, information, and data that lead to personal conviction. You become convinced of the truth. It leads to much more than the gathering of facts; you build and stake your life on those words. They become the foundation that holds your life secure, the wheels that enable you to travel to heaven and back, and the cool water that quenches your thirst in a dry land.

"Reproof" is the warning—"Watch out on this one"—element. This hits you over the head and in the heart. It not only tells you something is wrong, but the "yes, I agree" response echoes in your heart. If teaching is mental, reproof strikes the conscience. It tells you what's wrong and seeks to get you back on the right path.

"Correction" involves the volitional element, the will. It tells you how to get back on the path and how to stay on it. Thus, the Bible not only tells you what's what (teaching), what's wrong (reproof), but how to get it right (correction).

Finally, "training in righteousness." That's the practical process of running the player through the plays so that he or she can use the principles in any and every circumstance. Not only does the Word of God teach, rebuke, and correct you, but it's like the training manual complete with coach, team, and equipment. It doesn't just tell you what to do, but the supernatural element of the resident Holy Spirit makes it possible for you to do things as God gets directly involved with your life through the Word.

That's ultimately the miracle of Christianity. It's not dos and don'ts. It's not a list of rules. It's not even a manual to help you get your life together. It's a love relationship with God who seeks to bring the best into your life.

In my first book, *A Place to Stand,* I told about a boy learning to bat on a Little League team. Millions of boys have done that. But what if you had the greatest coach in history whose goal was to teach you to hit any kind of pitch that ever came across the strike zone? What kind of coach would he be?

First of all, he'd teach you. He'd show you how to get up to the plate, how to stand, how to swing the bat. Then he'd start hurling, slow and easy at first, but eventually he'd throw everything he could—curves, sinkers, forkballs, knucklers—to teach you how to hit in any and every situation.

The second thing he'd do is warn you about the danger spots, what to look for. He'd show you what the bad balls look like, what to avoid, and how not to get suckered into the wrong pitches.

After that he'd correct all the wrong habits you might develop. He'd show you the right way, the best way to swing. He'd get that dip out of your back leg, help you to choke up according to your size and weight, and correct any problems with your step into the ball.

Now all that would be great. What more could you expect of a coach? But there's still the last thing Paul mentions: "training." Now you might think that just means going over those other three steps, running through the paces.

But that's not all of it. Imagine that that coach can get down inside of your body and actually bat the ball through you. Imagine that he can energize you, strengthen you, help you, guide you every step of the way as he himself would do it, right inside of you. Not him standing on the outside watching. Not him just telling. But him right there in your own body. Now that would be some coach!

But that's what Scripture teaches about how the Bible and the Spirit of God work in us. He trains us in righteousness by being there with and in us every step of the way.

A Man Of God

Notice then the goal: to make a person a "man of God," that is, God's man or woman for all situations of life—God's representative.

God wants to make us much more than good, decent people. His goal is to make us little facsimiles of Himself. One day one of the angels might be talking to the Lord, "But I don't understand, Lord. This characteristic of Yours, can You show me it in daylight?"

"Sure," the Lord says, and He points to you: "Watch her. She's a perfect example of what I'm like."

That's what God is working toward.

Thoroughly Equipped

But then notice the results: that the person of God may be "thoroughly equipped." That's complete training. Every element is taken into consideration. Every possible situation is discussed and planned for. It all is included in one package. There are no false starts, no incomplete uniforms. "Equipped" carries with it the idea of being furnished. You've got every piece in place. Nothing's missing. You've got all the machinery you need to get the job done.

When a person is thoroughly equipped he's ready for anything. No problem, no situation, no circumstance can throw him. He's ready.

Reader's Digest once carried an interesting blurb about a lady who went to a specialist about an operation. When she arrived for her appointment, she found the young surgeon sitting at the receptionist's desk deeply engrossed in a book. He didn't hear her come in, so she cleared her throat, trying to see what he was reading. It was a Bible. She was a little astonished, and asked, "Does reading the Bible help you before or after an operation?"

The doctor looked up and quietly said, "During."

What a poignant story! But that's precisely what the Bible is for: not before or after, but *during*—whatever you're experiencing. You read it before to get equipped. You read it after to make sure things went according to specs. But it's during—the problem, disaster, crisis, or need that you have now—that all the equipping is for.

For Every Good Work

And finally, the overall aim: the doing of good works. That is going through this world and leaving heaven's mark on every person and thing you touch. Leave it a better place than you found it. Make the opportunity, and take the opportunity. Leave no job undone.

That's what the Bible wants to do in your life—in every nook, cranny, facet, drawer, pitcher, and pot of your being. It wants to infuse and infect everything.

Remember the story of the *Mutiny on the Bounty?* But do you know what happened after the mutiny? Captain Bligh and the few sailors still loyal to him were set into the lifeboats. They survived and returned to England. Finally an expedition was sent out to capture and punish the mutineers. Fourteen men were captured and punished. But nine had escaped to a distant island where they formed a colony with some of the natives, leading lives of debauchery. They learned to make whiskey from native plants. This soon led to their ruin. Rampant disease, killing, and immorality decimated their ranks. There was continual strife among the men and they killed one another off fighting over the women.

Eventually, every one of the original natives were dead and all the white men except one, Alexander Smith. After so much havoc and sin, he discovered a Bible in an old trunk and began studying it. He had never read it before. He believed it though, and began to apply it. He taught classes to the women and children.

It was twenty years before a ship ever found that island. What they discovered there though, was not a colony full of immoral, murderous people. They found a utopia. The people were living in harmony, decency, prosperity, and peace. There was no crime, no disease, no immorality or indecency, no insanity or illiteracy.

Why? Because they had been taught, rebuked, and corrected by the Word of God until they were trained in righteousness. They were *delighted by discipline*. The same thing can happen to all of us. If we'll only start. When? How about today?